2 95

KEEPING MARINE FISH

KEEPING MARINE FISH

Graham Lundegaard

BLANDFORD PRESS
POOLE · DORSET

First published in the U.K. 1985 by Blandford Press,
Link House, West Street, Poole, Dorset BH15 1LL.

Copyright © 1985 Blandford Press Ltd.

Distributed in the United States by
Sterling Publishing Co., Inc., .
2 Park Avenue, New York, N.Y. 10016.

British Library Cataloguing in Publication Data

Lundegaard, Graham
  Keeping marine fish.
  1. Marine aquariums
  I. Title
  639.3'42   SF457.1

ISBN 0 7137 1507 3 *(Hardback edition)*
ISBN 0 7137 1694 0 *(Paperback edition)*

Typeset by Megaron Typesetting, Bournemouth.

Printed in Great Britain by R.J. Acford, Chichester

CONTENTS

ACKNOWLEDGEMENTS

The many individuals and organizations who have offered their help and advice with this book are too many to mention individually, but I am grateful to them all. I would like to extend my especial thanks to the following: Ivor and Jean Wilder (The Aquatic Centre), Eric W. Sauerman (Penn Plax Plastics), Nick Fletcher (*Practical Fishkeeping Magazine*), P.E. Johnson (Thorn EMI Lighting), Richard Sankey (Tropical Marine Centre), Norbert Tunze (Tunze Aquarientechnik) and Chris Rawlings (Aqua Magic).

I would also like to thank Miss Anita Lawrence for the line drawings, Tunze Aquarientechnik for the photographs featured in Figures 1, 30 and 39 and Thorn EMI Lighting for providing the reference for Figure 21.

Graham Lundegaard

INTRODUCTION

So you are thinking about keeping marines. Perhaps you have kept fresh-water fish for some time but feel that they are a little plain compared with the dazzling variety of marine life. You may have been put off by tales of woe told by people who have lost a tankful of fish overnight. Maybe you have never kept so much as a goldfish in your life. If this is the case then you have probably been awestruck by a beautiful display of marine life in a public aquarium or, perhaps, a friend's fish tank, Whatever your reason, this book will tell you how to set up a living piece of coral reef in your home – successfully.

A marine aquarium is a thing of great beauty. The hobby is both compelling and absorbing. Keeping marines is also very educational, for all ages. There is no single science or art involved, but rather a combination of things. You will learn a little chemistry, a bit of physics, a sprinkling of marine biology and, above all, you will appreciate the wonder and beauty of the creatures that inhabit the oceans of our planet.

It is true that, until fairly recently, keeping marines has been fraught with problems. The toxic tank syndrome, whereby fish die within hours for no apparent reason, has been the bane of marine aquarists for years. Now, for the first time, the nature of the problem can be revealed. This book will ensure that almost anyone can keep a healthy, problem-free marine aquarium. Like many things, it is easy when you know how. And now we do know how. We have learnt from the failures of others in the past, great strides forward have been made in recent years and now keeping marines is easier than ever before. Do things slowly and patiently, and you will not go wrong.

For those of you who have kept fresh-water fish before, the basic principles are the same. Those of you who have not done so may have an advantage in that you will not tend to keep marines in the same way as fresh-water fish – a mistake often made!

Fresh-water tropical fish come from lakes, ponds and rivers. In these environments the water quality may vary considerably. Heavy rain will dilute the chemicals in the environment with pure water. Droughts will cause pure water to evaporate, concentrating the minerals and elements in the remaining water, thereby making it more dense and less pure. Because of the constant changes to which they are subject, fresh-water tropical fish have evolved to cope with a great variety of conditions. Hence, if a fresh-water aquarium gets a little neglected from time to time, it is unlikely to do the fish any harm, due to their ability to adapt. They are, in fact, remarkably tolerant.

The oceans of the world, you could say, are a different kettle of fish! Here conditions never vary. The environment is incredibly stable. The water chemistry fluctuates by only infinitesimal amounts. Even heavy rains are quite literally a drop in the ocean and cause no appreciable difference. The conditions around coral reefs are the most stable on earth and because of this the greatest profusion of life occurs in these areas.

Keeping a marine aquarium involves striving to achieve conditions so stable that marine life will flourish. It may sound impossible but, with the new understanding of the aquarium environment, it is not only possible but quite straightforward and easy! The quality and stability of the marine aquarium in your home is the science of the art.

Happy fishkeeping!

1
THE SEAWATER ENVIRONMENT

Everyone must have had a taste of sea water at some time – an accidental mouthful whilst swimming perhaps. It does, of course, taste salty and is often referred to as salt water rather than sea water. In fact, ordinary table salt, sodium chloride, forms the major part of the dissolved substances that make up sea water. However, it is no good mixing up a bucket of tap water with a handful of table salt and putting marine fish into it! There is rather more to sea water than that.

CHARACTERISTICS OF SEA WATER

Constituents

Sea water is in fact remarkably complicated stuff. It probably contains all the naturally occurring elements found in nature. I say probably, not certainly, because some of these elements are present in such tiny amounts as to be undetectable by scientific analysis.

The greatest bulk of sea water consists of pure water, 95% of good old H_2O. It is the remaining 5% that is so important.

Sodium chloride makes up the bulk of this, about 3%. Yet this is not a very accurate way of looking at things as, when sodium chloride is dissolved in water it splits into *ions* of about 2% chloride and 1% sodium. Confusing, isn't it?

Probably the simplest way of looking at the compounds that make up sea water is to break them down into their smallest constituents – elements – and, instead of referring to percentages, to refer to concentrations as parts per million or p.p.m. This is simply a finer scale, percentage is parts per hundred and becomes difficult when referring to very small amounts.

Let us now look at the major components of sea water on a parts per million scale:

Table 1. *Major components of sea water*

Element	Concentration (p.p.m.)	Element	Concentration (p.p.m.)
Oxygen	857,000	Magnesium	1,350
Hydrogen	108,000	Sulphur	885
Chlorine	19,000	Calcium	400
Sodium	10,500	Potassium	380

All of these substances are absolutely essential to support life. Hydrogen and oxygen are obvious because they make up water itself. Chlorine and sodium make ordinary salt. The remaining four elements are necessary for the cells of living organisms to function properly. A fish placed in a solution of sea water with, say, potassium removed would die quite rapidly.

Now we come to the minor elements. These are present in quite small quantities but make up a significant proportion of sea water:

Table 2. Minor components of sea water

Element	Concentration (p.p.m.)	Element	Concentration (p.p.m.)
Bromine	65	Boron	4.6
Carbon	28	Silicon	3
Strontium	13		

Bromine is useful to a small extent as a pH buffer, although sea life could probably survive without it. Carbon in the form of bicarbonate is the major compound necessary for a high and stable pH (pH is the degree of hydrogen ions present; see p. 13). Silicon is used only by certain diatoms, a simple form of algae, although it is suspected that certain animals may also use it. Boron and strontium are not known to be used. Indeed, some authorities consider that the presence of strontium is actually harmful, despite the fact that it occurs naturally.

Finally we come to the trace elements. These elements make up less than 2 p.p.m. yet some are essential.

There are also up to thirty other elements present in microscopic amounts. Those marked with an asterisk are known to be essential to life of some sort. Others, such as caesium, seem to perform no useful function at all. Of the important trace elements, most are needed by algae or bacteria. Fish seem able to get all the elements that they need from their food, whereas algae, and creatures such as anemones that have algae living inside them, have to get their supply from the water in which they live.

Do not be concerned if you find these longs lists of complicated names confusing. Fortunately you don't have to know any of them to keep a marine aquarium and they are included merely to show how complex sea water is.

Specific gravity

All these complicated chemicals, when dissolved in water, have the effect of making it more dense. You can measure the density, or specific gravity (SG), with a device called a hydrometer; indeed, you may have used one for wine-making. It is a simple device that floats in the water and on its side is a scale of specific gravity. Pure water has a specific gravity of 1.000. Add salt to water and it becomes more dense, causing the hydrometer to float higher in the water.

Table 3. *Trace elements in sea water*

Element	Concentration (p.p.m.)	Element	Concentration (p.p.m.)
*Fluorine	1.4	Uranium	0.003
*Nitrogen	0.5	*Manganese	0.002
Lithium	0.18	Vanadium	0.002
Rubidium	0.12	Caesium	0.0005
*Phosphorus	0.07	Silver	0.0004
*Iodine	0.06	Yttrium	0.0003
Barium	0.03	*Cobalt	0.00027
Aluminium	0.01	*Selenium	0.00009
*Iron	0.01	Thorium	0.00005
*Molybdenum	0.01	Lead	0.00003
*Zinc	0.01	Mercury	0.00003
*Nickel	0.0054	Lanthanum	0.000012
Arsenic	0.003	Gold	0.00001
*Copper	0.003	*Chromium	0.000005
*Tin	0.003	Scandium	0.000004

Natural sea water has a specific gravity of between 1.023 and 1.027, depending on where it is taken from. It is usual for aquarium water to be maintained at SG 1.020 to 1.022, i.e. 1.020 to 1.022 times the density of pure water. This is all very convenient for the marine aquarist because here we have a simple and inexpensive way of determining how much salt is dissolved in the aquarium water.

The density of water varies with temperature. Hot water expands and becomes less dense than cold water. It is therefore necessary to measure the specific gravity at a given temperature. Most hydrometers are calibrated at 24°C (75°F), which is the temperature at which we need to keep our fish.

You may be wondering why aquarium sea water is kept at a lower specific gravity than natural sea water. This is because the metabolism of sea water fish is such that they have to work much less hard in water of a lower density. Also, certain parasites seem to fare less well in a lower-density environment.

It is not critical; an aquarium can be maintained at any specific gravity between 1.020 and 1.025. What is important is to keep it as constant as possible. Remember we are striving to keep the environment as stable as we can for our marine aquarium.

Why should the specific gravity vary at all? You might think that the salt, once in the water, has nowhere to go. The answer is that the salt stays put but the water evaporates, leaving the salt behind and thus making the remaining water more salty and dense. It is a simple matter to replace evaporated water with ordinary tap water and thus achieve a fairly stable balance.

Figure 1. The discerning aquarist can keep water quality very close to that found in nature by using sophisticated instruments such as this Tunze conductivity meter.

This procedure is quite adequate for most purposes but it is possible to maintain the specific gravity at an absolutely precise and stable level by using advanced equipment. An electroconductivity meter (Figure 1) measures dissolved salts on a scale of microSiemens (μS). To give an idea of the sensitivity of such a device, 1 unit of specific gravity is equivalent to approximately 2,500 μS. Such instruments have been available for use in fresh water for some time, but only recently has technology produced a meter capable of measuring the conductivity of sea water. Obviously there is no point in using this instrument if buckets of tap water are sloshed into the tank to replace evaporated water. Tunze produce an electroconductivity meter and an associated device called an osmolator (see p. 65).

This is a marvellously sensitive piece of equipment that automatically replaces water lost through evaporation. If a spoonful of water evaporates, the osmolator pumps back in a spoonful of fresh water.

The aim of installing such elaborate and sensitive equipment is to try and achieve the ultimate stability that prevails in the ocean. If this goal is reached, then marvellous things start to happen; a lush growth of seaweed and chemically pure water can make it possible to keep the most delicate of creatures.

As I have already said, a bucket of tap water is quite adequate for most purposes, but for those that must have perfection then the osmolator is another step forwards.

Hydrogen ion concentration (pH)

The pH is a measurement of the number of hydrogen ions in a solution or, put more simply, of the acidity or alkalinity of a liquid. (Scientifically-speaking, this is not a completely accurate definition as it is possible to have different alkalinities at the same pH.)

The scale of pH runs from 1 to 14: 1 is extremely acid, 7 neutral and 14 very alkaline. For the technically minded, each whole pH unit represents a 10-fold change in hydrogen ions, making the scale logarithmic.

Sea water is rather alkaline, with a pH of about 8.3. In the marine aquarium, pH is kept in the region of 8.1-8.4. Once again, this is not absolutely critical but it should be kept as constant as possible. Fluctuating pH means that the plants, bacteria, fish and invertebrates have to adapt constantly to a changing environment. Means of measuring pH and keeping it stable, or *buffering*, as it is called, are described on p. 38.

SEAWATER, NATURAL OR SYNTHETIC?

Some of us are fortunate enough to live near the sea and therefore have a ready supply of sea water for our aquaria. However, great care must be taken when using natural sea water for a number of reasons.

a) Inshore water may be quite heavily polluted by industrial waste and natural organic material. Unless the water quality is known to be good, it is advisable to collect sea water some distance away from the shore by means of a boat.
b) The natural sea water will contain millions of planktonic creatures that begin to die the moment the water is removed from the sea. Unless the water can be used within a hour or so it will become polluted with decomposing plankton.
c) Tropical marine fish have no resistance at all to marine disease organisms native to Britain, so, unless you live in the tropics, even fresh sea water is unsafe to use.

Fortunately there are ways round these problems. One method involves leaving the sea water to stand in the dark for a month or two. During this period, organic matter is used up by any surviving plankton. The plankton then die through starvation and this gives rise to an increase in bacteria, as these feed on the remaining debris. Eventually these bacteria also starve and the inert debris will fall to the bottom of the container. It is then a simple matter to siphon off the now sterile sea water. It is important that this entire process takes place in the dark because, if there is any light, algae will grow and become food for other organisms.

This may sound rather tiresome and there is another, much quicker, process – sterilization. This can be achieved by adding calcium hypochlorite or sodium hypochlorite to the sea water until the chlorine level reaches 5 or 10 p.p.m. These chemicals and the chlorine test kit necessary to determine the levels are available through swimming pools' supply companies. The next thing is to remove the chlorine by adding a dechlorinator, such as sodium thiosulphate (photographers' hypo) until no trace of chlorine remains. Alternatively, chlorine can be forced out of solution by vigorous aeration for a few days.

Ozonizers and ultra-violet sterilizers (pp. 51 & 57) may be used to sterilize sea water but care should be taken as both devices are only powerful enough to kill smaller organisms. If either device is used it should be run for several days in the hope that prolonged treatment will eventually kill even large organisms.

All three methods of treating sea water are bound to alter its chemical make-up to some extent but all are tried and tested and appear to produce water of sufficient quality to support life.

Most of us do not live near to the sea and have to rely on synthetic sea salt. In fact, many people living right next to the sea use artificial sea salt because it is so simple to use.

Artificial sea salt is produced by a variety of manufacturers and comes in the form of a dry mix of the necessary chemicals. All that is needed is to add the approximate quantity of tap water and aerate it for a few hours. A quick check with the hydrometer at the correct temperature and, hey presto, instant sea water. If the hydrometer reading is low, add more salt; if it is high, add more water.

TAP WATER

A word about tap water here. You would assume that, if tap water is good enough to drink, then it must be good enough for fish. This is sometimes the case but not always. An obvious thing to watch is old lead piping and new copper piping. Both will release some traces of the metal into the water so it is wise to run the tap for a few minutes. Not so obvious is water coming out of the tap that is unfit to keep fish in. I have recorded instances of ammonia levels well past the fatal limit to fish, in water straight from the tap. This occurrence may be due to a breakdown at the water treatment station, or the the addition of chloramine.

Traditionally, water for human consumption has been treated with chlorine. Quite high levels are used at the treatment works but the water is then dechlorinated with chemicals such as sulphur dioxide before it passes into the distribution system. A low level of chlorine is maintained to keep the water in the pipeline sterile before it reaches the tap. This chlorine level seldom exceeds 0.3 p.p.m. and tap water can be added directly to a marine tank in small quantities.

If the water in a tank is being completely replaced, the chlorine should be removed by aerating the water for a few days or by treating it with a commercial brand of dechlorinator.

As water authorities are forced to use more polluted water and to pump it over longer distances, other means of sterilization have been developed. In some places, tap water may be treated with chloramine, which is a more stable form of chlorine and may be pumped for many miles without losing its disinfecting qualities. Good news for us but bad news for our fish!

Chloramine is produced by mixing chlorine with free ammonia. In water for human consumption, levels of either chemical seldom exceed 0.4 p.p.m. However, treatment works have found monochloramine to be the most desirable form of chloramine and this form can become unstable. When it does so, it becomes trichloramine, which has an unpleasant smell, and to prevent this happening, the works add further free ammonia to the water to keep the monochloramine stable. The resulting chemical brew not only has the 0.4 p.p.m. ammonia present in the chloramine, but the extra amount that has been added as free ammonia. The total amount of ammonia can therefore be as high as 1 p.p.m.

It is easy to check for chloramine by means of an ammonia test kit and as the sources of water supplies often vary, it is a good idea to check tap water for ammonia whenever it is used for fish.

The problem is that chloramine is very stable. Heavy aeration will dispel it but it takes at least a week, preferably two. If a dechlorinator is used, the chlorine is neutralized but the ammonia is left behind. It is possible to remove this ammonia by filtering through a resin called *zeolite*, but this resin is only effective in fresh water so it must be used before salt is added.

Probably the easiest way to remove chloramine is through a special tap water filter, such as the Mayrei filter (Figure 2). This contains a special highly activated carbon that absorbs the chlorine. Initially some ammonia will pass through the

Figure 2. Tap water may be safe for human beings but it is sometimes fatal to fish! A good tap water filter can remove most of the troublesome chemicals.

filter but soon a catalytic reaction occurs and the ammonia is transformed to nitrogen, making the water quite safe.

An alternative is to have a large reservoir used for mixing up batches of sea water. A small box filter containing activated carbon is used to filter tap water in the reservoir for a few days. It should be removed when salt is added.

It is a good idea always to filter tap water as the water authority often treat water with all sorts of chemicals without notice.

It is not so unusual, at least in England, to have a high nitrate content in tap water. If nitrate levels exceed 30 p.p.m. then it will become difficult to keep very delicate creatures, such as live corals and butterfly fish.

Sometimes water purification plants treat water with chemicals such as pyrethrum to kill off any crustaceans in the pipelines and some treatment works use aluminium or iron sulphate as a flocculant. You can either cross your fingers and hope all is well or contact your water authority and ask their advice.

The precautions which can be taken may be summarized as follows. Metals from pipework are disposed of by running the tap for a few moments. Ammonia and nitrite can be checked for with aquarium test kits. If either is present the water is not safe to use.

Nitrate is more of a problem. Its presence is due to excessive use of fertilizers for farming and the problem will continue to grow. If there is a high nitrate then try to locate a safer source of supply. There are some ion-exchange resins that will absorb nitrate, but failing this, it is something that will have to be put up with.

Pipes are usually treated in the summer and some water authorities may publish warnings in the local press, so keep an eye open. Most treatments and some contaminants may be removed by passing the tap water through activated carbon which absorbs chemicals from the water. Commercially available tap water filters are fine and probably do us human beings some good as well.

2
FISH AND INVERTEBRATES

Before you rush out and buy an aquarium in which to put your sea water, think carefully about what it is you actually want to keep: fish, invertebrates or both. It is important to decide before buying any equipment or aquariums, as the requirements for these three options differ slightly.

What is the difference between fish and invertebrates? Everyone knows what fish are of course, but what about invertebrates, or 'inverts' as they are referred to in the trade? By definition, invertebrates are creatures without a backbone. They come in myriads of shapes, sizes and colours and include such creatures as shrimps, crabs, starfish, sea cucumbers, anemones, sponges, corals and even octopuses.

Whatever you choose to keep, the basic requirements are the same: heating, lighting, filtration and, of course, sea salt and test kits.

FISH-ONLY SYSTEMS

Let us look first at a fish-only system. Lighting is not critical but it should be bright enough for you to see the fish and for the fish to see where they are going. It is thought that vitamin production within the skin of a fish is stimulated by long-wave ultra-violet light. Too little is known at this stage to recommend the use of so-called 'black light' tubes, but it is sensible to try and provide something resembling the spectrum of light that the fish are used to. Natural sunlight tubes, such as Truelite or Tropical Daylight, are useful for this purpose.

Filtration is the most important thing because the quality of the water that your fish will live in depends on it. It is wise to buy the finest filtration equipment that you can afford. The water that is pumped through the filters needs to be turned over at a higher rate than for an invertebrate tank. A good protein skimmer is a valuable asset which will remove the bulk of fish waste completely from the system before it reaches other filters and before the fish 'stew in their own juice'.

The aquarium for a fish-only system should be as large as you can afford. The reasons for this are that the larger the volume of water the more stable the water chemistry and the happier the fish. The limiting factors are the cost of the filtration for a large tank and the amount of space available in which to put it. A tank less than 130 l (30 gallons) is not suitable. In Europe, aquariums of between 250 and 1000 l (80 and 200 gallons) seem most popular.

A tank of 500 l (110 gallons) may sound awfully big, but bear in mind that the recommended stocking rate is initially 1 cm of fish per 7 l of water (1 in per 4 gallons), rising to 1 cm per 3.5 l (1 inch per 2 gallons) after the system has been running for 6 to 12 months. This means that in an aquarium holding 130 l (28½ gallons) the most you could ever keep would be, say, four medium-sized fish.

Advanced aquarists get round this problem by having a separate reservoir underneath the main tank and circulating water between the two. This increases the maximum stocking level of the display tank and also has the advantage that much of the filtration and heating equipment can be hidden in the reservoir.

I should explain here that *fish centimetres* refer to the distance from the tip of a fish's nose to the base of its tail but excluding the tail itself. If an aquarium is said to have a stocking capacity of say, 40 cm (about 16 in), then it would be possible to keep twenty fish 2 cm (¾ in) long or ten fish 4 cm (1 ½ in long). It is merely a rule of thumb but works well. There are extremely complicated formulae that allow stocking capacity to be worked out exactly, but, believe me, the fish centimetre rule is much easier!

INVERTEBRATE AQUARIUMS
Now for the invertebrate aquarium (Figure 3). Here lighting is critical. Many invertebrates have algae living inside them from which they benefit. They have the unpronounceable name of 'zooxanthellae'. These algae need bright light to survive; without good lighting they die; without zooxanthellae the invertebrates die.

For a tank 30-50 cm (12-20 in) deep, 25-30 watts of fluorescent light will be needed for each 1000 cm^2 (1 ft^2) of surface area, in order to keep most invertebrates.

Figure 3. One of the author's invertebrate aquariums containing live corals and algae. Such a set-up requires good lighting and water quality.

For certain live corals, such as *Goniopora*, and for seaweeds like *Caulerpa*, even more intense light is needed. Spotlights and mercury vapour lamps are useful for picking out areas of an aquarium where these are to be kept.

Not all invertebrates need such bright light. Shrimps and crabs, for example, do well even in dim lighting. However, good lighting is still worthwhile, even in this situation, as it has other secondary benefits. Good lighting promotes a lush growth of algae on which some fish and invertebrates can graze. Algae also absorb many harmful substances from the water. If algae are present then it is probable that some planktonic life is present and this will provide food for filter-feeders, such as tube-worms and some corals.

Filtration is not quite so critical for invertebrates; most seem more tolerant of water conditions. Filters do not need to have such a high turnover as for a fish tank; say half to three-quarters of the power. High-powered filtration is not even recommended because it is likely to strip any plankton and food out of the water before it can be utilized by invertebrate life. A good protein skimmer is still of benefit however. By keeping the water free of organic fouling, even the most delicate life forms may be kept.

The aquarium itself need not be as large as a fish-only aquarium. It is almost impossible to overcrowd invertebrates. Indeed, it seems that the greater the variety of life, the better the system becomes. This is probably because a more natural balance is created and some invertebrates probably feed on the waste from others. A tank of between 100 and 200 l (26 and 52 gallons) is quite acceptable; A larger tank is even better but can be a little expensive to stock.

It is a good idea to buy as much 'living rock' as possible for an invertebrate aquarium. This is rock inhabited by thousands of microscopic creatures and a few larger ones visible to the naked eye, such as crabs, starfish, sponges, polyps and seaweeds. It provides food for many inhabitants of the aquarium and also contains useful bacteria that purify the water. In fact, it is possible to rely solely on living rock for filtration, but this is not normally recommended. The cost of the rock will depend on which part of the world you live. Air freight on lumps of rock is expensive!

It is possible to have a few fish in an invertebrate system. You should choose fish that are not prone to disease and are suitable companions to the invertebrates. Clownfish that live in anemones are almost a must with perhaps a few small wrasse.

MIXED AQUARIUMS

Any more fish than this and the system becomes a mixed tank, which is a different proposition altogether. A mixed tank can be defined as either an invertebrate system with a fairly high proportion of fish, or a fish system with at least one invertebrate. A mixed tank is the most popular set-up, particularly with beginners because they do not know any better. Unfortunately, it is the most difficult to manage.

The main problem with this system is disease. When fish get white spot or

Oodinium disease (note WHEN not IF!), it is necessary to treat them with a copper-based solution. Such cures are very effective but unfortunately they are poisonous to invertebrates. So if you treat the tank, the invertebrates will die and if you do not, the fish will die. You need only one invertebrate in a fish tank and you are in trouble! One peculiar exception to this is the humble hermit crab. This fascinating little creature is as tough as old boots and can resist almost anything – including copper.

If you must have a mixed tank, then read on. Firstly stop and think before buying any fish or invertebrates. Are they compatible with everything else in the tank? Large crabs eat tube-worms, butterfly fish will generally attack anemones, corals and tube-worms, some angel fish will eat polyps and sponges, sticky anemones will eat fish, cone shells can kill fish (and human beings!); the list is endless.

Lighting has to be good enough for the invertebrates. Filtration has to be good enough for the fish. The aquarium has to be large enough for both. In addition to these demands, some method of disease control is necessary. It is possible to fit ultra-violet sterilizers and ozonizers to the tank in the hope that this will prevent the transmission of disease. Ultra-fine filters, such as diatomic or cartridge filters, can be used to sieve out larger disease organisms.

A hospital or quarantine tank is most useful. When disease strikes, it is possible to remove the fish or the invertebrates to the quarantine tank so that the fish can be treated separately. If the main tank is treated with copper then it must be removed before invertebrates are re-introduced. Exchange resins, such as Polyfilter, are useful for this purpose.

Living rock is also a form of invertebrate life and so this is also not really suitable for a fish-only system. This is unfortunate as fish do markedly better in a community system containing living rock. It is feasible to have some living rock with fish because it is easier to look after if the main tank has to be treated. It can be stored in a bucket of sea water at the right temperature with just an air stone to keep the water circulating. It will soon recover when put back in the display tank but, again, all copper must be removed first.

3
THE AQUARIUM

Having decided what type of inhabitants your aquarium will house, you should have an idea of what size to go for. But wait a bit longer before buying your aquarium yet! Patience is one of the skills of keeping marines, so practise now by reading the book through before buying anything.

A major consideration is a space in which to put the tank. It is no good buying a 2 m (6½ ft) long tank only to find that it will not go through the front door, let alone fit in the lounge! Look for a suitable site first. It should be away from any kind of heating, such as radiators. It should not be placed near to a kitchen, where oily fumes from cooking could get to the tank. It should be placed where there is a convenient water supply nearby. Some sunlight can be of great benefit, particularly in an invertebrate tank containing corals and seaweeds. Be careful though; a couple of hours of sunlight is sufficient, otherwise the aquarium can quickly become overrun by too much algae and end up as an unsightly mess.

The stand or base unit on which the tank will sit must be of sufficient strength. (Water is surprisingly heavy: 1 m³ weighs about 1 tonne cf. 1 ft³ which weighs 65 lb.) If it is to be placed on floorboards then try to ensure that the joists run at

---

Table 4. Useful figures in calculating the weight and capacity of an aquarium

---

Metric

$$\frac{\text{Length} \times \text{Height} \times \text{Breadth (cm)}}{1\,000\,000} = \text{Volume (m}^3)$$

1 m³ of water contains 1000 l of water and weighs 1000 kg or 1 tonne.

Volume (m³) × 1000 = Weight (kg) or capacity (l)

Imperial

$$\frac{\text{Length} \times \text{Height} \times \text{Breadth (in)}}{1728} = \text{Volume (ft}^3)$$

1 ft³ of water contains 6.24 imperial gallons and weighs approx. 62½ lb.

Volume (ft³) × 6.24 = capacity (imperial gallons).

Capacity (imperial gallons) × 10 = Weight (lb).

1 imperial gallon = 0.83 US gallons.

21

Figure 4. An Aquadecor Highline Aquarium designed to take most of the filtration equipment within the integral canopy. This leaves the aquarium free from distracting equipment inside the tank itself.

right angles to the length of the tank so that the load is distributed. Do not worry unduly about floor strength; consider the weight of a bath for comparison. You may find the figures given on the previous page of use.

An attractive base may be made from decorative brickwork or the tank could actually be built into a wall or chimney breast. Remember to leave room for all the equipment that may be needed. Some space underneath is useful for power filters and air pumps. Much of the more modern equipment (Figure 4) is designed to sit above the tank, so leave plenty of headroom for this. If spotlights or mercury lights are to be used then even more headroom is required, as well as plenty of ventilation. There should be sufficient space to be able to get decorations and rockwork in and out and it should be possible to use a fishing net in the tank without too much obstruction.

Most aquariums are made from glass bonded together with silicon adhesive. This is immensely strong and watertight and has made the old metal-framed tanks obsolete, except in some special circumstances. If the aquarium comes with a metal hood then this should be heavily varnished to prevent corrosion.

Remember that some equipment is designed to fit above the tank so a hood can get in the way. If this type of equipment is to be used then it may be better to buy a special tank designed to accept it, or build a wooden top yourself.

It is, of course, possible to make an aquarium yourself. Glass and silicon are readily available but be warned – it is often cheaper to buy the finished product than the materials to make it. To make a professional-looking aquarium is very difficult and I have seen many sad attempts with out-of-square sides and silicon fingerprints everywhere! Home-made tanks often leak as well!

4

HEATING AND LIGHTING

Tropical marine fish and invertebrates come from the warm seas in and around the coral reefs. It is essential to keep them at more or less the temperatures to which they are accustomed. Marine life is, in fact, remarkably tolerant to temperature, considering the ultra-stable environment from which it comes. Temperatures of between 23 and 27°C (73 to 80°F) are quite suitable. The rule is to keep the temperature constant. A constantly fluctuating temperature will spell disaster to a marine aquarium. Diseases such as *Oodinium* and white spot thrive in such conditions and things are made worse because the fish are weakened.

HEATING

Heating in the aquarium must be adjusted to match or exceed the maximum temperature of the room in which it is situated. Otherwise a situation can occur whereby the temperature of the aquarium is raised during the day by the heat of the room but, at night, drops until it reaches the temperature at which the aquarium thermostat is set.

Aquarium heaters are available in a range of different designs but all are suitable, providing there is no metal in the casing. It is possible to use a separate thermostat wired in series with the heater. Both internal and external thermostats are available, the external type tending to be more reliable. The usual and simplest method of heating is to use a combined heater/thermostat (Figure 5). This has the advantages of being cheaper, more compact and much easier to wire than separate heaters and thermostats.

A possible danger with heaters and thermostats is that, sooner or later, they will fail and the tank inmates will either fry or freeze! The simplest and most effective precaution is to use two heater/thermostats, each of half the desired wattage. This way, if one fails 'off' the other should keep the tank temporarily warm enough and if one fails 'on' it should not have enough power to overheat the tank.

Whatever method is used, it is essential to check the temperature each day with an accurate thermometer. Alcohol thermometers can be inaccurate and mercury thermometers will poison a tank if broken. The safest and most accurate thermometer is the stick-on liquid-crystal type which adheres to the outside and reads the temperature through the glass. It is difficult to give precise guides to the wattage of heater to use in an aquarium of given size as much depends on the room temperature and make of device used. As a very rough rule of thumb, 1 watt of heating is needed per litre of water if the aquarium is situated in a warm room. It is not critical as thermostats will automatically compensate to a considerable degree and keep the water at a surprisingly constant temperature.

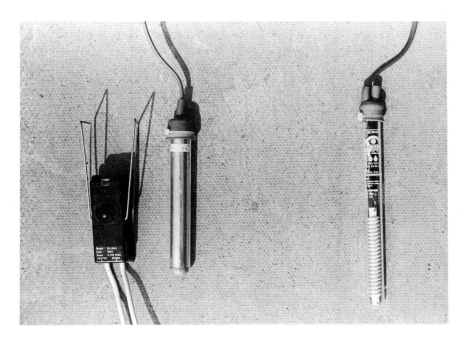

Figure 5. Water heating can be controlled either by a separate heater and thermostat (left) or by combined units (right).

If disaster does strike, it will do so when all the shops are closed. It is therefore not a bad idea to keep a spare heater/thermostat handy, bearing in mind the value of the aquarium inhabitants. If the worst comes to the worst, and a heater has failed 'off', it is possible to keep the aquarium warm by adding hot water (not salt water) carefully to the tank and insulating it by wrapping blankets around it. If a heater has failed 'on', the temperature should be lowered slowly by disconnecting the heater and perhaps adding a bag of ice cubes to the tank. Either way it is important not to alter the temperature suddenly and further stress the fish.

LIGHTING

The importance of lighting in the marine aquarium is often under-estimated. A rough guide to lighting has already been given in Chapter 3 but it will now be covered in greater detail.

There are several different types of lighting that can be used and a number of technical terms are necessary to understand them:

a) The *efficiency* of an electric lamp can be defined as the proportion of power consumed by the lamp that is actually converted to visible light. For example, an

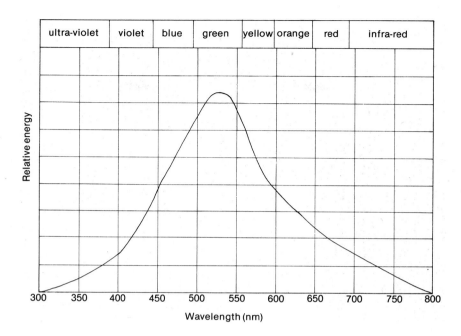

Figure 6. Sensitivity to light of the human eye. Plants 'perceive' light in a quite opposite manner.

ordinary electric household light bulb is very inefficient. Only 5-10% of the electricity consumed is converted to visible light. The rest of the energy is used to produce light in the infra-red end of the spectrum, beyond the range of human vision. This energy is radiated as heat and, as we all know, light bulbs can get hot enough to burn fingers! An efficient light source is one that uses energy to provide visible light with little heat.

b) The *efficacy* of a lamp is a guide to how bright a light source appears to human eyes for a given amount of power consumed. It is measured on a scale of lumens per watt. The human eye perceives the wavelength of 550 nm which is the yellow to green portion of the spectrum, to be brightest (Figure 6). Our perception of brightness falls off towards the red end of the spectrum on one side and the blue end on the other. Thus a 1 watt yellow lamp will appear much brighter to us than a 1 watt blue or red light. This can be taken to the extreme of ultra-violet and infra-red light that we cannot see at all, yet all generate, more or less, the same amount of radiation. This means that a lamp with a high efficacy value appears brighter to us than one with a low efficacy value. This does not necessarily mean that the light source is more efficient, it may be that the lamp with the higher value simply contains more yellow light than the other.

c) The *colour temperature* of a light is defined as the temperature, in degrees Kelvin, to which a black body must be heated in order to emit light of a given colour. It is widely used in colour photography. Daylight under an overcast sky has a colour temperature of 5500°K. Light of a higher value appears blue as under a cloudless sky. Light with a lower value appears to have a red cast, as in morning sunrise.

d) The *colour rendering* of light is the degree to which objects viewed under it appear to match their true colours as seen under daylight. For example, a light source with good colour rendering may illuminate a bouquet of flowers and they will appear the same colour as they would in daylight. A light of poor colour rendering would throw a coloured cast on the flowers making their colours difficult to discern.

e) The *colour appearance* of a lamp is the colour that it appears when viewed in daylight. For example, a household light bulb appears to give a yellow light when viewed in daylight.

Incandescent or tungsten lighting includes household light bulbs, tungsten striplights, spotlights and floodlights. The efficiency of these lamps is very poor as most of the energy is converted to heat rather than light, so they are expensive to run, although the initial cost is low. Efficacy values are around 10 lumens per watt for a bulb but as high as 20 for a spotlight, these being more efficient. The colour temperature is typically 2000°K, giving a reddish yellow colour appearance. Colour rendering is good and objects wil appear to be more or less their natural colour.

Household bulbs are not used much these days for aquariums. They are too hot and very inefficient. Small pygmy bulbs of around 8 to 15 watts can have their uses though. In the wild, marine creatures seldom if ever experience total darkness. In a mixed-community aquarium it is quite possible for a prize marine fish to accidentally blunder into an anemone, and quite literally meet a sticky end, if kept in total darkness at night. A low wattage tungsten light will provide a dull glow at night, so that the fish can still see where they are going.

Spotlights provide a bright focused beam of light and floodlights give a wider spread. Both are useful for keeping corals and anemones that require intense light. They should be of the heavy-duty type so that they do not smash if accidentally splashed with water. As these lamps produce a great deal of heat, it is essential to position them some distance from the water surface to prevent overheating. Adequate ventilation must also be provided. They have the advantages of being relatively cheap and producing a pleasant rippling effect in the aquarium.

Tungsten quartz-halogen lamps of 50 to 100 watts are occasionally seen mounted above an aquarium. These lamps are more efficient than the ordinary tungsten bulbs but usually have to be run with a transformer, making them economically unattractive.

High-pressure mercury lamps (Figure 7) are used extensively in England and Germany but have not yet caught on in the USA. These lamps are run in series with a ballast unit, a bit like a fluorescent light. The cost compares well with fluorescent

Figure 7. High pressure mercury lamps are gaining popularity because of their high intensity output and very low current consumption.

lighting. The older type of mercury lamp was not very suitable for aquariums because the colour rendering was poor. The modern de luxe type of mercury lamp gives good colour rendering with a slightly orange appearance. They are extremely efficient and have an efficacy value of around 50 lumens per watt. Due to the rather unnatural spectrum these lamps produce, it is not applicable to suggest a colour temperature.

Mercury lamps offer an efficient, compact and relatively cool light source. There are two types available: an elliptical bulb and a reflector floodlight. The elliptical bulbs are quite compact but are obviously better if used with some type of reflector. A mirror or white-painted board will serve to reflect the light down into the aquarium. The reflector lamps are better because all of the light is directed downwards at source. The disadvantage of the reflector lamps is that they are comparatively bulky and rather more expensive. De-luxe colour-rendering mercury lamps are only available in 80 and 125 watt versions, giving the equivalent of 300 and 450 watts of tungsten lighting respectively. Higher-wattage mercury lamps do not have such good colour rendering but they are sometimes used in very large aquariums. They are available up to around 1000 watts, which is equivalent to an almost unbelievable 4000 watts of tungsten light!

A variation of the mercury lamp is the metal-halide lamp. These lamps are incredibly efficient with an efficacy value of around 80 lumens per watt. Colour rendering is even better than for mercury lamps and a more natural spectrum is produced. These lamps are ideal for aquarium use but are not often seen for two reasons. The cost is around four times that of standard mercury lamps and, in addition to a ballast unit, an electronic ignitor is also needed, making the control gear complicated and expensive. For those who seek the ultimate, this type of lighting is worth considering.

Both types of mercury lamp mentioned have an advantage over other forms of lighting due to the manner in which the light gradually reaches full brightness over a period of several minutes after being switched on. This means that fish are not suddenly shocked when the lights are turned on but can adjust as the light intensity gradually increases.

Fluorescent strip lights are used extensively for aquariums and it is true to say that most tanks are illuminated solely by this type of lighting.

Fluorescent tubes are available in a great variety of sizes from a 15 cm (6 in), 4 watt tube, up to 240 cm (94½ in) at 125 watts.

Not only are there a great range of sizes available but there are also at least thirty different types of tube, all giving different colour rendering and different spectral distributions. Most fluorescent tubes are very efficient and all have more or less the same wattage output. It is interesting to note that the efficacy value varies considerably, even though the efficiency is the same. For example, a De Luxe Warm White tube has an efficacy of about 50 lumens per watt but a Grolux tube has an efficacy of only 20. This is simply because the De Luxe Warm White tube has a considerable amount of green and yellow in its output, so our eyes perceive it as being very bright. The Grolux tube, on the other hand, has almost no yellow or green but instead has a large amount of blue and red present, which our eyes do not perceive as being so bright. Therefore to our eyes, the Grolux tube seems only half as bright as the other, even though both have the same wattage output.

So much for how we see light, but what about the inhabitants of our aquariums? There is little doubt that fish see things in much the same way as human beings so lighting for a fish-only tank presents little problems. But what about invertebrates? You may recall that certain invertebrates contain an algae from which they benefit; it is this algae that needs the light. How do algae perceive light? Well of course algae have no eyes or brain but they do react to different colours of light. Algae contain chlorophyll which converts light into energy, enabling it to grow. This process is known as photosynthesis, the details of which will not be given here. What is of interest to the aquarist is that chlorophyll reacts most strongly to light at the red and blue sections of the spectrum and reacts least to light of the yellow and green parts of the spectrum (Figure 8). It would seem then that algae 'perceive' light in the opposite manner to ourselves. To algae, red and blue seem brightest and yellow dimmest. To human beings, yellow seems brightest and red and blue dimmest.

It is therefore tempting to illuminate an invertebrate aquarium with light in the red and blue wavelengths. This is, in fact, the thinking behind Grolux tubes. These lamps produce a spectrum that matches the needs of plant life almost exactly (Figure 9). Unfortunately, there are some disadvantages in relying solely on this

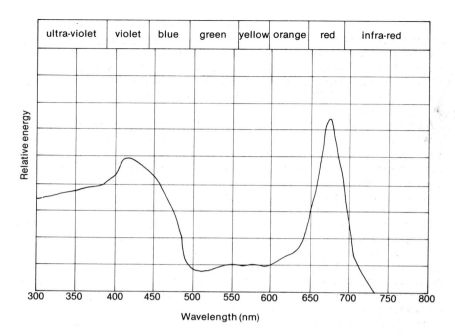

| ultra-violet | violet | blue | green | yellow | orange | red | infra-red |

Figure 8. Absorption of light by plants.

type of illumination. For one thing, the colour rendering of this type of lighting is poor. The colour appearance is purple and this tends to give an unnatural look to an aquarium. For fresh-water fish, the effect is quite pleasing, as reds and blues are highlighted and the fish seem unnaturally colourful. Marines are much more vividly coloured to start with and there is little point in enhancing this further, although this would doubtless appeal to some. Another point is that these lamps appear to us as being rather dim and a marine aquarium looks its best when brightly lit. Sealux tubes partially overcome these problems by not only peaking at red and blue in the same way as Grolux, but also by giving out more yellow and orange. This results in a whiter-looking light.

It is interesting to consider the natural environment of the invertebrates and seaweeds. Colours are filtered out of sunlight as the depth of water increases. Red is the first to go, so, unless the life form comes from relatively shallow water, it is unlikely to receive any red light anyway. On top of this, experiments have shown that algae will thrive even under spectra that are not well matched to their needs, providing that the light is bright enough.

So where does this leave the aquarist? Confused probably! The best thing seems to be to illuminate the aquarium with light that is similar in appearance to natural daylight. Some additional red and blue can be provided with Grolux tubes. Possibly

29

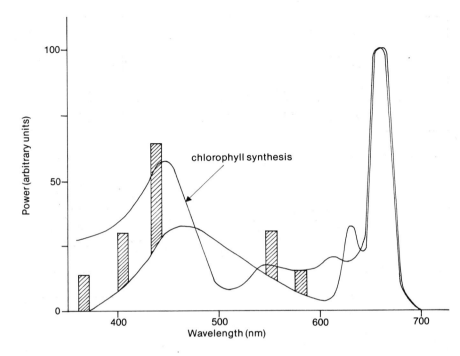

Figure 9. This graph shows how closely the Grolux energy emission curve follows the chlorophyll synthesis curve of the majority of plants. Grolux is the lamp expressly designed for this purpose.

tungsten strip lights are of some benefit by providing the deep red and infra-red that is usually lacking in fluorescent lights.

There are a large number of tubes that give a spectrum similar to daylight but some thought must be given to colour temperature. The brightest-looking fluorescent lights are high in yellow and tend to have a colour temperature considerably less than natural daylight. Such tubes tend to give the aquarium a yellowy dingy appearance as if the water were very old. Natural daylight has a colour temperature of 5500°K. Fluorescent tubes with a colour temperature of less than 4000°K are not recommended. Tubes with a colour temperature of 5000-7000°K are ideal; the higher the value, the colder blue the tube will appear.

The charts overleaf show the spectral distributions and colour temperatures of a number of lamps suitable for aquarium use. Probably Tropical Daylight, Naturalux, Sealux and North light are most suitable. A combination of different types of light (Figure 10) is quite acceptable. A mixture of daylight-type tubes will give a wider spectrum than just one type. A proportion of Grolux lighting may be

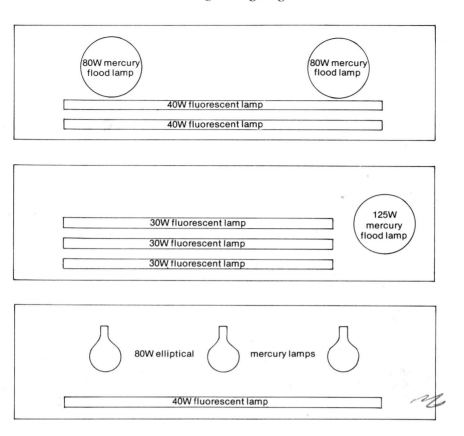

Figure 10. Three possible lighting combinations for an aquarium approximately 1.5 m long by 0.5 m wide (5 × 1½ ft) suitable for light-loving invertebrates.

of benefit, particularly in deep tanks where red will be filtered out, giving the aquarium a greenish cast.

If tungsten strips are used, they should account for no more than 10% of the total wattage of light. Tungsten spotlights should be used with care to pick out areas of interest or light-loving creatures.

Mercury lamps provide a compact and intense light source. A 125 watt lamp is equal to 2.5 m (98½ in) of fluorescent tube or four 100 watt tungsten spots. Although corals and anemones thrive under mercury lighting and the colour

Figure 11 (overleaf). Spectral distribution charts of various light sources suitable for aquarium use.

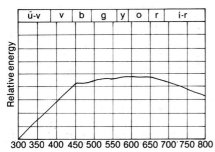

Natural sunlight
Efficacy: N/A
Colour temperature: 5500K
Colour rendering: excellent

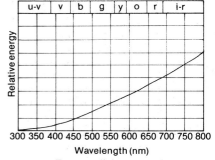

Tungsten light
Efficacy: 15
Colour temperature: 2800K
Colour rendering: good

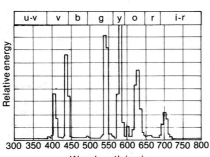

De luxe mercury lamp
Efficacy: 50
Colour temperature: N/A
Colour rendering: good

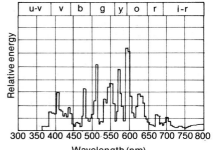

Metal halide
Efficacy: 75
Colour temperature: N/A
Colour rendering: excellent

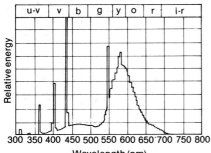

Warm white fluorescent
Efficacy: 67
Colour temperature: 3000K
Colour rendering: good

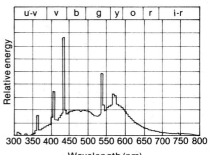

Tropical daylight fluorescent
Efficacy: 48
Colour temperature: 6500K
Colour rendering: excellent

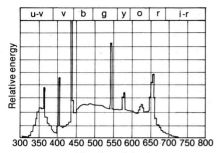

Artificial daylight fluorescent
Efficacy: 30
Colour temperature: 6500K
Colour rendering: excellent

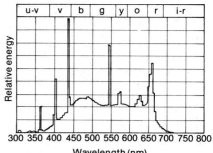

North light fluorescent
Efficacy: 42
Colour temperature: 6500K
Colour rendering: excellent

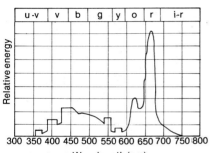

Grolux fluorescent
Efficacy: 20
Colour temperature: 10 000K
Colour rendering: fair

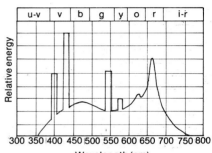

Sealux fluorescent
Efficacy: 40
Colour temperature: 5326
Colour rendering: good

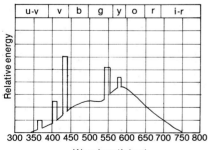

Naturalux fluorescent
Efficacy: 55
Colour temperature: 5150K
Colour rendering: excellent

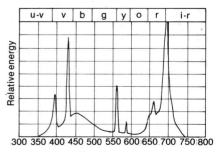

Aquarilux fluorescent
Efficacy: 22
Colour temperature: 10 500K
Colour rendering: fair

u-v=ultra-violet v=violet b=blue g=green y=yellow o=orange r=red i-r=infra-red

appears natural, this light does, in fact, produce a fairly spiky and unnatural spectrum. It may be wise not to rely solely on mercury lamps but to supplement them with one or two fluorescent tubes.

A luxmeter can be of help in determining the correct level of illumination for various types of marine life. This is a rather expensive light meter but some more modern aquarium shops will hire them out. If you can get one, the information below in Table 5 will be of help.

Table 5. Optimum light levels for marine organisms

Organism	Light levels in lux (approx.)
Most corals and green algae, including seaweeds	12000-16000
Brown and red algae, bubble corals and most anemones	6000-10000
Sponges, leather corals and gorgonians	2000-5000

It is possible to calculate the lux output for different types of lighting but in practice this can be misleading as it is difficult to take into account light lost and gained. For example, half the available light is lost through inadequate reflectors, some is lost through dirty cover glasses, still more through the filtering effect of dissolved organic compounds in the aquarium water. To offset this, a certain amount of daylight is sure to fall on the aquarium. Probably the best method is the age-old science known as trial and error!

Some aquarists experiment with sunrise and sunset systems, giving the aquarium a more natural form of lighting. This is easily achieved by having different lamps on individual time switches. If mercury lamps are used then these should come on first as the light output builds up gradually. Three time-switches, switching on at 1 hour intervals is quite effective. Similarly they may be turned off at 1 hour intervals in the evening.

The length of time that the lights are on for is known as the *photoperiod*. It should be 12 to 16 hours for algal growth; anything much longer than this is detrimental.

5

THE PURPOSE OF FILTRATION –
THE NITROGEN CYCLE

As mentioned earlier in this book, tropical marine fish and invertebrates come from water that is incredibly stable and pure. They have no mechanism to adjust to a changing and unstable environment because in nature they simply have no need to do so. In a closed aquarium environment, fish will pollute the water in which they live with their own waste products. Indeed, without filtration, marines will poison themselves within days of being put in an aquarium.

In nature, the poisonous waste excreted by fish and invertebrates is broken down by bacteria that utilize it for food. In the aquarium, we have to try and imitate nature by providing filtration. The various filters available and their functions will be described later (see Chapter 6). The most important of these filters is the biological filter, which utilizes the helpful bacteria found in nature to dispose of the toxic waste products of the aquarium inhabitants.

THE NITROGEN CYCLE

The sequence of events by which these bacteria break down waste products is known as *the nitrogen cycle* (Figure 12) and it is the most important aspect of keeping marines in an aquarium and, on a larger scale, is of equal significance in the open sea.

Figure 12. The nitrogen cycle. Because the aquarium is rich in oxygen, anaerobic bacteria capable of utilizing nitrate are normally in the minority. Oxygen-loving aerobic bacteria create nitrate much faster than it can be removed, so nitrate usually accumulates.

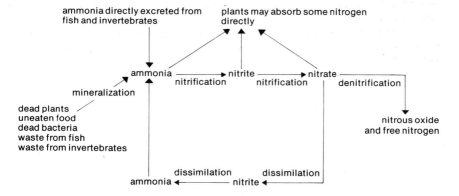

In the aquarium, biological filtration is provided either by an under-gravel filter, an external canister filter or a trickle filter. The principle is similar in each case. Water containing oxygen and a supply of nutrients, in the form of waste matter, is allowed to flow over grains of gravel or a purpose-made biological medium. Bacteria colonize the granules by creating a layer of slime around them in which they live. As the water passes over the granules, bacteria take in oxygen and digest the waste matter for food. The water leaving the filter is purified because the bacteria have removed the waste matter from it.

The first stage in this process is the excretion by fish and invertebrates of organic waste into the environment. This waste is added to by decaying uneaten food, dead animals and dead bacteria. The nature of this waste is somewhat complicated and it consists of amino acids, proteins, urea and other compounds. Several different groups of bacteria are able to utilize these organic compounds and reduce it to ammonia. Bacteria capable of using organic products as food are called *heterotrophic* bacteria. These bacteria are also capable of other functions but it is not necessary to go into this too deeply here. The process of converting this organic waste to ammonia is called *mineralization*.

The resulting ammonia is added to by more ammonia excreted directly by invertebrates and by fish, *via* their gills. Ammonia is extremely toxic to fish.

The next stage in the process is *nitrification*, in which ammonia is broken down to form nitrite; in turn, nitrite is broken down to nitrate. Bacteria capable of utilizing these inorganic chemicals as food are called *autotrophic* bacteria and are probably the most important found in nature.

Again, there are several species of bacteria capable of nitrification but two are considered to be the prime species involved. Ammonia is utilized by *Nitrosomonas* bacteria, which convert it to nitrite, which is far less toxic. *Nitrobacter* bacteria then take over and convert the nitrite to nitrate, which is almost harmless. Without this fortunate sequence of events it would be impossible to keep marines.

What happens to the nitrate? It seems that, wherever there is a potential food source, nature has some bug or beasty capable of utilizing it as food. There are several bacteria that can use nitrate but most of them are anaerobic, i.e. they can normally only operate in an environment lacking in oxygen. Most parts of an aquarium are aerobic and contain plenty of oxygen so nitrate-reducing bacteria are not as prolific as nitrifying bacteria, so nitrate always accumulates in most aquaria.

Nevertheless, some anaerobic bacteria do exist in the aquarium and these do feed on nitrate. This process is called *dissimilation*. The end product of dissimilation depends on which bacteria are present and, in turn, this depends on subtle differences in the environment. Many anaerobes are capable of reversing the nitrogen cycle and convert nitrate to ammonia. Fortunately these bacteria do not normally proliferate, except in an overcrowded and under-oxygenated aquarium. A more useful form of bacteria comprises those that can reduce nitrate to free nitrogen gas and nitrous oxide, which is released back into the air. This process, which gets rid of nitrate completely, is called *denitrification*.

In most aquariums, nitrification exceeds denitrification and so nitrate accumulates. Nitrate is not toxic at normal levels and does not present a problem because regular water changes will keep it down to acceptable levels. New aquarium systems are now available that provide optimum conditions for denitrifying bacteria and, if these are used carefully, it is possible to maintain an aquarium at almost zero levels of nitrate. Although nitrate is probably not toxic, it is desirable to keep the level as low as possible because nitrate is only present in the ocean in minute quantities. The object of a marine aquarium is to keep conditions as close to nature as possible.

THE MATURING PROCESS

In a completely new aquarium there is a time lag between each stage of the biological process. Bacteria will find their own way into an aquarium but it is possible to speed things up by seeding the system with a handful of dirty gravel from an existing mature set-up.

If fish are introduced into a new and immature aquarium, they will begin to produce ammonia which is highly toxic. The ammonia level will rise gradually over the first couple of weeks as there will be insufficient bacteria to break it down. Gradually bacteria will reproduce and feed on the toxic ammonia to produce the less toxic nitrite. Ammonia inhibits the ability of bacteria to reduce nitrite to nitrate, so the nitrite level will begin to rise also. By now the bacteria are multiplying as fast as they can and begin to use up all the available ammonia. Now

Figure 13. The maturing cycle. Note that nitrite continues to build up until the inhibiting ammonia is competely broken down.

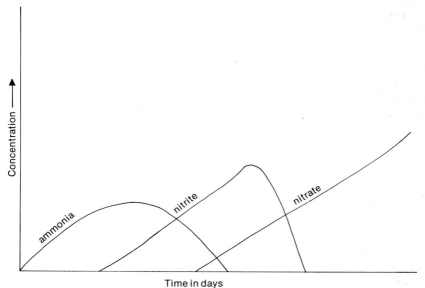

the ammonia level in the aquarium will begin to drop. Without the ammonia to inhibit them, the bacteria will start to break down the nitrite to nitrate and so the nitrite level suddenly falls, leaving only harmless nitrate. This is called the *maturing process* (Figure 13).

You will notice that there is a rise in toxic ammonia followed by a rise in nitrite, which is also toxic but not as much so as ammonia. In the early days of marine aquariums, this process was not understood and fish in a new tank always died. It was called the 'new tank syndrome' and was just something to be put up with. Now that the maturing process is understood, it is easy to mature a tank without loss. It can be done either by introducing one or two hardy fish that will withstand ammonia and nitrite, or by using a commercially available rapid-maturing agent. Either way, ammonia and nutrients are provided for the bacteria and the system will mature.

The maturing process can be monitored with aquarium test kits. With a good quality nitrite test kit, the aquarium water may be tested every day or so. The nitrite level will be seen to rise from zero to 10 or 20 p.p.m. and then, almost magically, it will disappear completely overnight. It is also possible, though not essential, to monitor the initial rise in ammonia.

When the nitrite level has collapsed it is safe to assume that the necessary bacteria have established themselves and it is safe to stock up the tank. Each time a new specimen is introduced, the bacteria will have to increase to cope with the new load on the system. Because of this, the tank must be stocked slowly, reaching its maximum stocking capacity over a year.

HYDROGEN ION CONCENTRATION (pH)

Natural sea water has a pH of 8.3 and we must strive to keep it somewhere near this level in a marine aquarium. Biological filtration overall produces nitric acid (Figure 14), which tends to lower the pH. It is important to prevent sea water from dropping below a pH value of 8. Fortunately sea water contains *buffers* which prevent pH drop (Figure 15). As acid is added to the water from the biological filter, so buffers combine with the acid and neutralize it.

By definition, buffers are substances that prevent additions of weak acids or alkalis from altering the pH value. Sea water has quite a strong buffering effect and pH will not drop appreciably whilst these buffers are present. The main buffer in sea water is carbonate.

Normally, the action on a buffer in sea water is one-sided in that acid is constantly generated by the action of the biological filter. If left unchecked, the buffer capacity of the sea water will become exhausted and pH will then drop.

The buffer capacity of an aquarium can be increased by using mineral carbonates in the form of gravel and rocks. Tufa rock consists of almost pure calcium carbonate and provides an excellent aquarium decoration with good buffering potential. Dolomite consists of calcium and magnesium carbonate and is sometimes used as a gravel, particularly with under-gravel filters. Coral sand, sea shells and corals also provide some buffering capacity. As acid is added, so the mineral

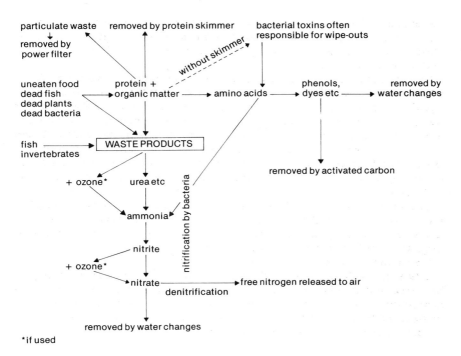

Figure 14. The nitrogen cycle in a system using biological filtration.

Figure 15. Stylized representation of how pH is maintained until the buffer capacity is depleted.

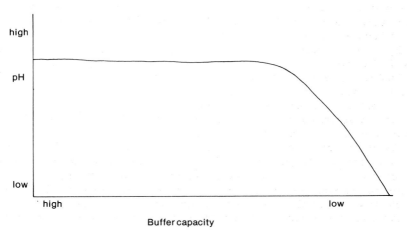

carbonates dissolve and form new bicarbonate and carbonate ions, ready to neutralize the acid.

Mineral carbonates cannot be relied upon for complete buffering. Bacterial slimes and calcite crystals will grow over rocks and gravels, making them increasingly ineffective with time. Eventually pH will drop and preventive action must be taken.

The routine maintenance of a marine aquarium should include changing 20% of the water each month with a fresh sea salt solution. This in itself is often sufficient to maintain adequate buffering, but if pH does drop then action must be taken.

If pH drops to 8 or below, then the addition of 1 level tablespoonful of sodium bicarbonate per 50 l (11 gallons) of aquarium water should be sufficient to increase the pH over a period of 2 or 3 days. Sodium bicarbonate is available as ordinary baking soda but make sure it is pure! Sodium carbonate can also be used but great care is needed as its action is immediate and can cause a sudden rise in pH which is detrimental to both fish and filter bacteria. Remember – keep things stable!

Persistently low pH can indicate an overstocked and under-filtered aquarium, or an unfavourable reaction between a particular brand of sea salt and local tap water. To check the sea salt, mix up a fresh solution at the usual SG and aerate it for 24 hours, then check the pH. Depending upon the chemistry of the mix, it should be between 8.2 and 9. If it is low, then it is worth trying a different brand of sea salt.

6
FILTRATION EQUIPMENT

By far the most commonly used filter is the under-gravel filter. Indeed, freshwater aquarists often rely on it as the sole means of filtration. It harbours useful bacteria that remove toxic fish waste and by so doing provides *biological* filtration. It also strains out small particles of waste matter (particulate waste) from the water and so provides *mechanical* filtration.

BIOLOGICAL FILTRATION

An under-gravel filter (Figure 16) consists of a perforated plastic plate that lies on the bottom of the tank. It should cover at least three-quarters, and preferably the whole, of the bottom of the aquarium. Connected to this plate, or plates, are uplift tubes that rise from just below the under-gravel filter to the water surface. A layer

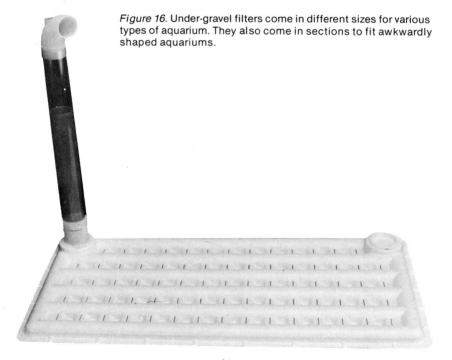

Figure 16. Under-gravel filters come in different sizes for various types of aquarium. They also come in sections to fit awkwardly shaped aquariums.

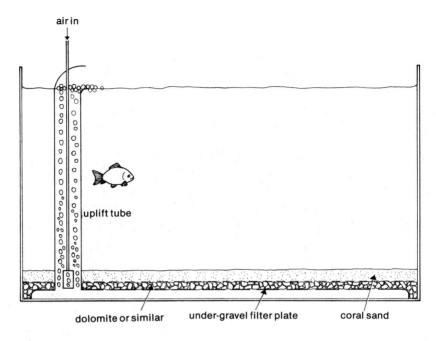

Figure 17. An air-operated dual-layer under-gravel filter system.

of gravel is placed on top of the filter and water is pumped through the gravel, through the under-gravel filter, through the uplift tube and back into the tank.

The filter can be powered by either an air pump or a water pump. An air pump can be utilized by running a length of air-line tube from the pump and threading it down the uplift tube where it terminates level with the filter plate. Air is driven down the air line and bubbles back up the uplift tube expelling air and water at the surface. The operating principle is a little less obvious than may first appear. It looks as if the air bubbles are pushing the water up the tube with them but, in fact, because the mixture of air and water in the uplift tube is less dense than the surrounding water, water is drawn in at the base of the tube to try and displace it (Figure 17). An air pump has the advantage of being cheap and efficient. The disadvantage is that such pumps tend to be rather noisy and can be most distracting when trying to view your favourite television programme!

Compact and powerful submersive water pumps (Figure 18) are available which simply plug into the top of an uplift tube and pump water directly through the filter. Most can be fitted with an optional venturi device which enables the pump to blow out some air with the water so that oxygenation is provided as well. Such pumps are available in a large range of powers for filters of varying sizes and turnovers. The advantage of water pumps is that they are virtually silent in

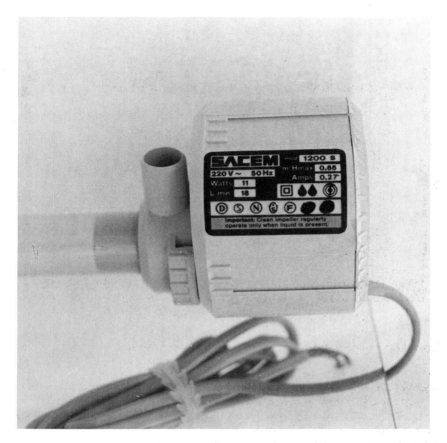

Figure 18. Submersible water pumps called power heads are available to plug directly into under-gravel filters. They are virtually silent-running and can pump more water than an air-driven filter. The pump illustrated can pump 18 l (4¾ gallons) a minute and is capable of driving a filter bed of considerable size.

operation; also some can pump more water than an air pump. The disadvantage is that they tend to be more expensive.

The nature of the filtration depends to a great extent on what filter medium is used.

Biological filtration is optimized by giving bacteria a very large surface area to colonize (Figure 19). This is achieved by using a porous angular gravel or sand. The more irregular and porous the medium, the greater its surface area. Smaller grains will also offer a greater surface area in a given volume than large grains. Against these factors must be offset a couple of others. Grains of gravel that are *very* irregular will not fit neatly together and a lot of empty space will be created

43

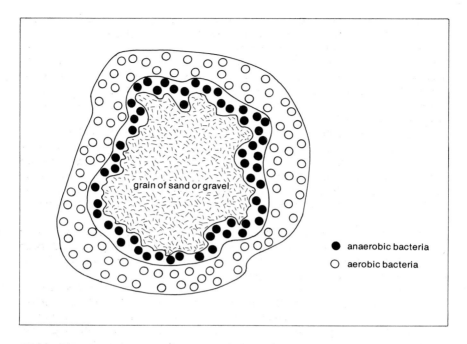

Figure 19. Bacterial activity around a grain of gravel in a biological filter. Anaerobes may exist only in the central region where the oxygen is depleted.

between them; this space cannot be utilized by bacteria. On the other hand too fine a grain of gravel will not allow enough space between grains for water to flow. Ideally gravel should be rough and porous, with a particle size of about 2 mm ($7/10$ in) and some pH buffering ability. Coarse coral sand has all these properties.

As water flows through the gravel bed, bacteria colonize its surface and break down passing waste matter and absorb oxygen from the water. Detritus, formed from particulate waste and debris from bacterial activity, collects between the grains of gravel. This is also colonized by bacteria so that old dirty filters offer better biological filtration than new clean ones. Most bacteria colonize the first few centimetres of filter bed where food and oxygen are abundant. In the lower depths of the filter bed, bacterial activity diminishes as supplies of nutrients and oxygen decrease. The optimum thickness of filter bed for biological filtration seems to be about 7-10 cm (3-4 in), although deeper beds are not harmful.

MECHANICAL FILTRATION

Mechanical filtration in an under-gravel filter is incidental but beneficial. As water is pumped through the gravel bed, particulate waste is strained out by a number of mechanisms. Particles larger than the gaps between gravel particles are simply sieved out. Finer particles may stick together (flocculate) and again become to big to pass through. Some particles collide with the gravel with sufficient force to become glued to its surface by impact. Some particles come to rest in areas of the filter bed where there is little or no water movement. Finally, some waste is electrically attracted to gravel grains of opposite charge. The performance of this apparently simple function is therefore quite complicated! Under-gravel filters, therefore, keep the water pure by breaking down dissolved waste products and clean by sieving out dirt.

The flow rate through an under-gravel is also important. Optimum flow rate for a well-stocked fish system is in the region of 50 l per m² of filter bed per minute (1 gallon per ft² per minute). For an invertebrate system, this may provide too powerful a mechanical filtration and food and plankton may be removed. The flow rate may be reduced by as much as half in such situations, as the biological load is much reduced in an invertebrate aquarium and such powerful filtration is unnecessary.

The filter bed itself usually consists of two separate layers of substrates. Coral sand is often so fine that it will fall through the slots in the filter plates and so, to prevent this, a coarse layer of filter medium should be placed beneath the coral sand and kept separate from it by a perforated plastic mesh.

The base material needs to be coarse enough to allow a free flow of water and should preferably have some pH buffering capability. Dolomite, calcite, crushed shell and coral gravel are all suitable. The pH buffering capacity is often over-emphasized. Although most materials will initially give good buffering, they eventually become covered by organic growth or crystals of insoluble compounds. The pH buffering is therefore at its best only during the first few weeks of use.

Where two layers of filter material are used, roughly 45 kg per m² (10 lb per ft²) of *each* filter material are necessary. For a single layer of filter material, roughly 65 kg per m² (15 lb per ft²) are needed.

Under-gravel filters have the advantages of being cheap, efficient and reliable. Disadvantages are that they take up a lot of aquarium space, bacteria consume much of the available oxygen from the water and they get rid of nothing, merely convert it to harmless detritus and nitrate.

Another method of biological filtration that is rapidly gaining in popularity is the trickle filter (Figure 20). Water is first mechanically pre-filtered and then sprayed onto porous granules suspended above the water in troughs or cartridges. Because the bacteria are only kept moist by a trickle of water, there is far more oxygen available to them from the air. This causes a much thicker film of bacterial slime to develop on the granules than would be possible in a submerged filter.

Trickle filters are now considered superior to under-gravel filters because of the following advantages: more efficient biological filtration, greater compactness than under-gravels, consumption of oxygen from the air not the water. Disadvantages are: bacteria are more easily damaged by medication added to the water and by toxic fumes from the air; the turnover of water is slower, meaning that the filters are slower to react to sudden surges of pollution, and more head room is needed above the water surface.

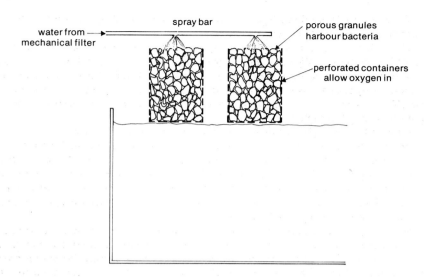

Figure 20. The principle of the trickle filter system.

PROTEIN SKIMMING

Biological filtration is essential to rid the aquarium of the toxic waste produced by its inmates. Its disadvantages are that it causes a steady decline in pH, a gradual rise in nitrate and the production of organic dyes that turn the water yellow with age. It is obviously an advantage if the bulk of waste products can be removed from the water before biological filtration. A good protein skimmer will remove up to 80% of organic waste products which reduces the load on the biological filter by a corresponding amount.

A large proportion of organic wastes in the aquarium consist of *surfactants* (surface active agents). These compounds are attracted to any interface between air and water. A protein skimmer works by producing millions of fine air bubbles around which surfactants can accumulate. The resulting organic sludge is then skimmed off and discarded. A protein skimmer is a unique aid to filtration in that it removes waste from the water completely whereas other methods strain out or adsorb debris. It should be noted that a skimmer will only work in sea water. In fresh water it is completely useless.

The efficiency and sensitivity of a protein skimmer is limited by the size and number of air bubbles produced and the length of time that the bubbles are in contact with the water. The more bubbles there are, the greater the surface area for surfactants to attach to. The finer the bubble, the more bubbles per volume of water. The greater the length of time the bubbles are in contact with the water, the more surfactants will attach to them.

There are basically three types of protein skimmer: through-current, counter-current and powered venturi jet skimmers.

Through-current skimmers are the simplest and least efficient. They are generally capable of providing adequate skimming for aquariums of 50-100 l (10-20 gallons). The skimmer consists of a clear plastic cylinder of about 10 cm (2 in) diameter which is suspended vertically in the tank. At the bottom of the cylinder, a wooden air diffuser is attached. At the top of the cylinder, above the water surface, a scum collection cup is attached.

Air is driven through the wooden diffuser and produces a column of foam in the cylinder. The foam rises above the water level but not enough to flow into the collecting cup. If protein is present, it is attracted to the surface of the air bubbles and rides up the cylinder with them until they burst at the surface of the foam column. Here protein accumulates and forms a secondary layer of oily foam which is pushed up by pressure of the foam column and overflows into the cup. It is then a simple matter to occasionally empty the cup.

Some of these skimmers have a water outlet nozzle just below the water surface. This enables water to be drawn up the foam column and returned to the tank. In practice, it is not necessary to pump water through such a skimmer because protein wil be drawn to the foam column by diffusion. No protein is present within the skimmer yet the surrounding water contains protein. Protein is therefore drawn into the skimmer to maintain equilibrium.

A counter-current skimmer (Figures 22 & 23) is an improvement on this device and is generally capable of skimming an aquarium of around 135 l (30 gallons) if

Figure 21. A Tunze high-pressure protein skimmer suitable for aquariums of up to 1000 l (264 gallons) capacity.

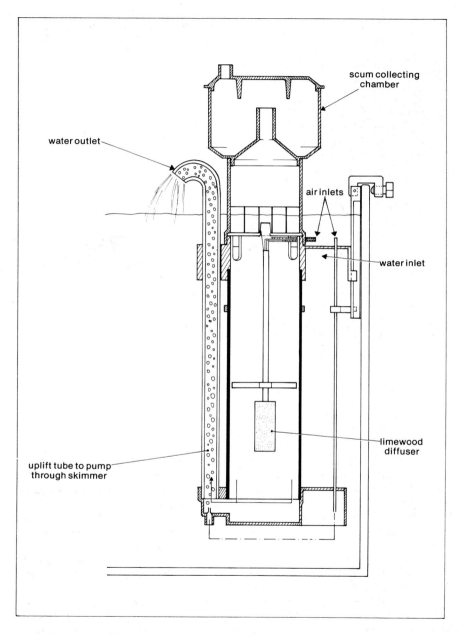

Figure 22. A Sander counter-current protein skimmer.

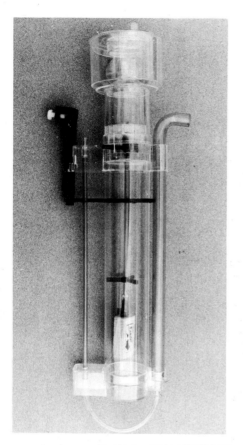

Figure 23. A Sander counter-current protein skimmer is a very efficient aid to smaller aquariums.

fitted inside the aquarium although there are more efficient external ones. This device is similar to the previous one except that water enters the foam column *via* holes in the cylinder situated just below the water surface. The water is pumped down *against* the flow of water and back into the tank. This is achieved by attaching an air-uplift tube or a water pump to the bottom of the cylinder which is otherwise sealed. This type of skimmer has the advantage that the air bubbles rise slowly against the flow of water and so contact time is maximized.

Counter-current skimmers are usually available in different lengths for tanks of different depths. The longest possible model that will fit in the tank should be used. The longer the skimmer, the longer the contact time.

The more efficient type of protein skimmer is undoubtedly the motor-driven venturi-jet skimmer (Figure 21). These are suitable for aquariums of 250 to thousands of litres (50 to thousands of gallons) capacity, depending on the power of the water pump.

49

They work by means of a water pump producing a high-pressure jet of water which is mixed with air in a venturi chamber. This results in millions of very fine air bubbles around which protein accumulates. The foam is directed into a chamber to maximize contact time and the resulting scum is collected in a removable cup.

The advantages of protein skimming are: a greatly reduced load on the biological filter, a slower decline in pH, a slower rise in nitrate and therefore a much more stable environment. The greatest advantage is, however, the prevention of the toxic tank syndrome, or wipe-out. (This is discussed in detail in Chapter 7.) The disadvantages are that skimmers can look unsightly and that they can remove trace elements bound to organic waste. It may be necessary to add trace element supplements if invertebrates and seaweeds are being kept.

ACTIVATED CARBON

Activated carbon is a black granular filter medium used in power filters (see p. 53) or simple air-driven box filters. It has the capacity to adsorb organic substances from the water and can be compared, to some extent, with protein skimming.

The first stage in the manufacture of activated carbon is to burn a suitable material in the absence of oxygen to form carbon or charcoal. Various materials are used such as wood, bone and nutshells. Different materials alter the characteristics of the finished product. The second stage is to heat the carbon to extremely high temperatures under pressure. The resulting granules of activated carbon are extremely porous, to the extent of 1 gm ($^3/_{10}$ oz) having a surface area of 1000 m² (10764 ft²).

Organic waste is adsorbed onto the surface of these granules. The greater the surface area, the more waste can be adsorbed.

Just how activated carbon works is poorly understood but it is remarkably effective. It can adsorb waste matter that even a skimmer cannot remove, including the dyes that make aged water yellow.

One problem with activated carbon is that, when its capacity is exhausted, it can no longer adsorb waste matter. When this point is reached it rapidly sheds its load back into the water with harmful effects. New types of carbon are now being developed that do not suffer from this characteristic.

Carbon filtration will make the water in a tank absolutely crystal-clear, even when viewed lengthwise. If continuous carbon filtration is used, it is important to replace the carbon the moment it becomes exhausted. If possible, view the tank end-on from time to time. The moment it begins to look slightly yellow and dingy, the carbon should be replaced. There is no set rule for the life of activated carbon because it depends on the loading of the tank and the amount and brand of carbon used.

Carbon can also be used intermittently, say every 3 or 4 weeks. In this case, a small amount of carbon should be used for 24 hours to clear the tank and then be discarded.

Carbon can remove substances that cannot be removed by skimming, but skimming can remove substances not removed by carbon. The two are probably best used together. If water can be protein-skimmed and then carbon-filtered, the carbon will not be wasted on removing matter that the skimmer can cope with.

The advantages of carbon are that it will keep an aquarium crystal-clear at reasonable cost. The disadvantages are that it must be replaced regularly, it will not prevent the 'toxic tank syndrome' and it will remove trace elements and vitamins from the water. The removal of trace elements is not a great disadvantage in a fish-only tank because fish are able to get all they need from their food. It is probably best to run a carbon filter continuously in a fish-only aquarium but only occasionally in an invertebrate tank, or where seaweeds are cultured.

Ion-exchange or absorptive resins are occasionally sold for sea water filtration. Most work to some extent but are not usually as good as carbon for removing yellowing and are usually more expensive. For technical reasons, such resins do not perform as well as they might when used in sea water.

OZONIZERS

Ozone is a gas produced by means of a device called an ozonizer (Figure 24). In the marine aquarium it is used to bleach the water, improve oxygen saturation, increase the redox potential, oxidize organic waste and, last but not least, to mildly sterilize. The ozonizer is therefore quite a useful little gadget to have!

An ozonizer contains a high-voltage transformer producing around 12 000 volts. This produces a high-voltage discharge, or corona, within a special chamber. An air pump is used to pump air into the ozonizer and it emerges as ozone gas.

Oxygen molecules normally consist of pairs of oxygen atoms, hence the chemical formula O_2. Ozone molecules have three oxygen atoms (O_3). Ozone is very unstable and always tries to revert back to oxygen and to do this the extra atom is used to oxidize another compound. Because of its high oxidizing potential, ozone is remarkably efficient at burning up any organic waste within the aquarium water, particularly the dyes that cause yellowing. As the excess single oxygen atoms are used up, free molecules of ordinary oxygen are produced and this increases the oxygen saturation of the water. This combined action increases the redox potential.

The redox potential is a rather technical term that describes the measurement of the efficiency of aquarium water to cope with organic loading. Redox potential meters are available but are quite expensive. Details will be discussed in the section on test kits.

Ozone also has the power to burn up most viruses and bacteria that come into contact with it. It can also immobilise some larger disease organisms by destroying the cilia with which they swim. The sterilizing potential of ozone is often overstated. At best it is a mild sterilizing agent but, by improving water quality, disease is less likely to be a problem.

Excess ozone in aquarium water can be damaging to the gills of fish and useful bacteria. Seaweeds such as *Caulerpa* are also easily killed by too much ozone. Because of this, ozone is usually contained within an ozone reactor. A protein skimmer serves this purpose admirably. In air-driven skimmers, ozone is pumped

Figure 24. A Sander ozonizer. When used properly, an ozonizer is a valuable aid to water management.

into the wooden air diffuser. In power-driven skimmers, ozone is mixed with water by the venturi jet. The reaction of ozone with water is therefore confined to within the protein skimmer.

When working with high levels of ozone, some residual gas may remain in the water leaving the skimming chamber. In such cases the water should first flow over activated carbon before returning to the aquarium. Carbon will convert any remaining ozone into oxygen. The reaction is catalytic and will not exhaust the carbon prematurely. Ozone can be used at a low level continuously, at a higher level after feeding or during the night, or just when the aquarium water becomes dingy or disease is a problem.

Ozone has an acrid pungent smell, particularly when used to excess. At very high levels, it induces depression, headaches, nausea and even vomiting. Most ozonizers for aquarium use cannot produce dangerously high levels but can cause discomfort if not used properly.

If the ozonizer is to be used continuously, or when people are likely to be in the same room, the adjustment knob should be turned up slowly until ozone can just be smelt, then turned back a fraction. In this way, all the ozone is used to oxidize waste products and there is no excess. This is quite an accurate test as human beings can smell ozone in minute quantities.

If higher levels are to be used continuously, then the ozone gas leaving the skimmer should be passed through activated carbon or ducted out of the room. Most skimmers have an outlet nozzle that will accept 9 mm (⅜ in) tubing that can duct the ozone outside.

Alternatively, the ozonizer can be wired to a time switch so that ozone gas is produced only at night when the room in which the aquarium is situated is not occupied. Time switches are also sometimes used to turn an ozonizer on for 3 hours after feeding, when the organic load is at its greatest.

A word of warning. Ozone oxidizes everything very efficiently and this includes plastics. What are skimmers made from? Yes, that's right, plastic! Excessive use of ozone will make the plastic brittle to the point where it cracks and disintegrates and so will almost certainly shorten the life of a skimmer.

High levels of ozone can cause a build-up of the gas within the canopy of the aquarium. If trickle filters are used, this build up can damage the nitrifying bacteria so care should be taken.

Ozonizers are calibrated in milligrams of ozone per hour. The calibration is usually very inaccurate but, as a rough guide, the following can be considered a starting point for a tank of 225 l (50 gallons) capacity:

a) Continuous use: 5-10 mg/hour.
b) After feeding: 10-20 mg/hour.
c) At night only: 10-15 mg/hour.

In cases of disease, up to 50 mg/hour but excess ozone should be ducted out or the room left unoccupied.

POWER FILTERS

A power filter consists of a simple canister filled with a filter medium and fitted with a water pump. The simplest type is the internal power filter. This consists of a small plastic canister containing a purpose-made foam insert. Water is drawn through the foam cartridge and pumped back into the aquarium by means of a water pump fitted to the top of the canister. The foam cartridge provides mechanical filtration by simply sieving out particles of debris. Biological filtration will also be provided in time once bacteria have become established within the cartridge. Particulate waste matter in a marine aquarium tends to be very fine so care should be taken to choose an internal power filter that does not have too coarse a medium otherwise debris will pass straight through.

Maintenance is limited to cleaning the cartridge every few weeks. This should be done by gently rinsing the filter sponge in warm sea water. (Cold tap water would destroy any useful bacteria established within the sponge.)

The advantages of internal power filters are that they are cheap and easy to clean. The disadvantages are that they take up room in the tank, are limited to only one type of filter medium, and bacteria are destroyed when the filter cartridge is replaced.

A more elaborate power filter is the external filter. This is similar to the internal one but sits outside the tank and, because it is outside, is fitted with a much larger canister. Water is drawn into the filter from one end of the aquarium, filtered, and pumped back into the other end of the tank.

The filter canister can contain filter medium of your choice. A great variety of material is available, including activated carbon, special biological material, exchange resins and coarse, medium and fine filtration materials. Some filters are fitted with a large foam cartridge with a hollow centre in which other materials can be placed.

A biological medium consists of chips of inert but very porous rock or clay. This provides an ideal attachment site for the bacteria that will colonize its surface. This medium will never need replacing and will seldom need cleaning so, if it is used, it should be placed in the bottom of the power filter. Be sure to choose a coarse material that will provide little mechanical filtration or it will clog up and prevent the filter working efficiently.

If activated carbon is used it should form the layer above the biological medium as it will not require replacing very often and provides some coarse mechanical filtration.

Where mechanical media are used, they should be situated in the top layers as they will require replacing most often.

It is not necessary to use a coarse medium if there are already other media below, as these will provide sufficient coarse pre-filtration. However, it is a good idea to have a layer of medium filter wool before a final layer of very fine wool to prevent premature clogging.

When choosing a power filter, it is wise to decide on one that has the inlet at the bottom of the filter container. Some are fitted with the inlet and outlet on the top and water is passed down the side of the canister through a special channel to the bottom. It is then forced up through the layers of medium. With some of the cheaper filters, it is possible for water to by-pass the filter material by leaking across the dividing wall between inlet and outlet. A filter with the inlet at the bottom cannot have this defect.

Be sure that the canister is sufficiently large to take the medium that you choose and remember that a large canister will need cleaning less often.

Finally, check that it is easy to clean out. The top should be easily removable yet secure enough not to leak when used. Some manufacturers produce in-line valves and couplers making it easy to shut off the water from the aquarium and remove the filter without flooding the carpet. Believe me, this is money well spent!

The advantages of an external power filter are that they can house more material, are very versatile and, because they are outside of the tank, do not take up valuable room in the aquarium. The disadvantages are that the pipework can be awkward and it can take quite some time and effort to clean out.

Also available is the diatomic power filter. This is an outside canister filter that has been specially adapted to use diatomaceous earth as a filter medium; some are dual purpose and can also be used with a sponge cartridge.

Diatomaceous earth is a very fine, chalky white material that consists of the skeletons of diatoms, which are microscopic algae. About 40 gm (2 tablespoonsful) of this powder should be placed in the filter canister. Instead of a sponge cartridge, a large perforated bag, looking like a giant tea bag, is inserted into the filter canister and the top is then secured. Water is siphoned into the filter from the tank as usual and the pump switched on. By a special set of valves, water is pumped around the filter in a closed circuit. The diatomic powder is swirled up and coats the sides of the bag. After a couple of minutes, the water in the canister becomes clear as all of the powder is now forced against the filter bag. The valves are now adjusted and water is pumped from the tank, into the filter canister, through the diatomic powder, through the filter bag and finally back into the tank.

The advantage of this type of filter is that it is capable of extracting particles so fine that some disease organisms, including those causing white spot, can be filtered out.

The disadvantage is that, because it is such a fine filter, it gets clogged up very easily; usually after about a week of use. A diatomic filter is perhaps best used only occasionally to fine-polish the water or to attempt to control the spread of disease.

There are a number of ways in whch a power filter can be used. It is possible, in some circumstances, to use a power filter as the sole means of biological filtration. Internal power filters do not normally provide sufficient biological filtration because they are so small so a large external filter must be used. As it is difficult to establish a sufficient number of bacteria in a power filter, quite large quantities of biological filter medium must be used. Coral gravel is useful as it does not clog very easily. A layer of filter wool may be placed on top as a mechanical medium to strain out any fine debris. Quite large power filters of considerable turnover are needed. It is better in most cases to use under-gravel or trickle filters for biological filtration and to use power filters mainly for mechanical or back-up filtration.

A power filter can be used to back-up under-gravel filters. In this instance the turnover does not have to be so critical. Turning over the same volume of water per hour that the tank holds will keep the water clear and remove some debris from the bottom. In order to have adequate power to whisk away all debris from the bottom of the tank, a turnover of between three and six times the tank volume per hour may be required.

When used with an existing biological filter, such as an under-gravel, it is rather pointless to put additional biological medium in the power filter, unless the tank is overloaded. Instead it is best to stick to activated carbon and mechanical media.

If the power filter is large enough, and the mechanical filter medium fine enough, it is possible to rely on the power filter as the sole means of mechanical filtration. In this case, it is possible to use a much coarser medium in the under-gravel filter. Coarse coral gravel is well suited for this purpose as it does not provide fine filtration. This set-up has the advantage that the filter bed will not become clogged up, because the power filter is taking care of all the debris.

A power filter can be connected to an under-gravel and thus provide the power to drive it.

If the inlet pipe of the power filter is joined to the uplift tube of an under-gravel filter, then the power filter will draw water through the filter bed, through the power filter and finally pump it back into the tank.

If fine gravel or sand is used in the under-gravel filter, it will provide both mechanical and biological filtration, so the power filter is best filled only with activated carbon.

If the filter bed consists of coarse coral gravel, then the power filter must contain

Figure 25. A power filter can be used to drive an under-gravel filter in reverse-flow mode. Care should be taken to use a power filter of sufficient turnover for the size of filter plate being driven.

some fine mechanical medium in order to keep the water free of particulate waste.

If the outlet pipe of the power filter is joined to the uplift tube of an under-gravel filter, then the power filter will pump water underneath the filter plate, through the filter bed and into the tank, where it will be sucked back into the power filter (Figure 25). This system is called a *reverse-flow* system.

If a fine material is used on the filter bed of a reverse-flow system, there is a danger that water will bubble through in just a few patches, leaving much of the filter bed unfiltered. This is caused by water taking the easiest route and forming miniature patches of quicksand. To avoid this, it is best to use a coarse material, such as coral gravel, which will diffuse the flow evenly.

A possible danger with reverse-flow and powered through-flow filters is that the power filter can get choked without being noticed. When this happens, the flow rate decreases and bacteria in the filter bed die and are replaced with dangerous anaerobic bacteria that will quickly poison the tank. A power filter should be checked often!

A power filter must be run for 24 hours a day. If it is turned off for more than an hour then the bacteria living inside the filter canister will die and anaerobic bacteria will take over. When the filter is turned back on, a couple of litres of toxin will be pumped back into the tank, killing everything. I once lost my priceless pair of breeding clownfish through just such an incident.

Where power filters are used to drive under-gravel filters, the turnover must be adequate to drive the filters at the rates previously stated (p. 45). Do bear in mind that manufacturers tend to quote the turnover of power filters very optimistically. Usually the output is measured with no medium in the filter canister and minimal pipework. The *actual* turnover can be half of the stated output. This is particularly true of the low-wattage power-saving motors that are designed to pump a high volume of water at a very low pressure. The slightest restriction will drop the flow rate considerably.

SURFACE SKIMMERS

A surface skimmer is a device designed to skim off from the water surface scum caused by bacteria and algae. These are usually designed to attach to the inlet pipe of a power filter, although some self-contained units are available.

Surface scum can be a real problem in a marine tank. Once present, it can be extremely difficult to get rid of. It cuts down light and reduces oxygen exchange at the water surface.

A surface skimmer has its inlet level with the water surface and skims off the troublesome film. It is a simple but effective device and well worth considering. Do not, on any account, confuse a surface skimmer with a protein skimmer. Both do completely different jobs.

ULTRA-VIOLET STERILIZERS

Strictly speaking, ultra-violet sterilizers (and ozonizers) are not filters because they do not actually filter anything out of the water but both have to be used with other pieces of filtration equipment and are therefore included in this chapter.

An ultra-violet sterilizer is a device designed to destroy free-swimming disease organisms in the aquarium. It works by producing powerful short-wave ultra-violet radiation capable of killing any organism, providing that the unit is sized correctly.

Only a very narrow band of ultra-violet light has the property of sterilization; its wavelength is 253.7 nm. A few units difference either side of this frequency dramatically reduces the sterilizing effect.

Light of this one special frequency has the ability to penetrate the walls of disease organism cells and destroy the DNA molecules at their centres. The amount of radiation needed to achieve this depends on the size of the cell. With larger organisms, the outer cells shield the inner ones and so the ultra-violet light has to be more intense.

At the heart of a sterilizer is a special ultra-violet tube. It looks like an ordinary fluorescent tube except that it has no white coating on the inside and is completely clear. Short-wave ultra-violet light cannot pass through ordinary glass so the tube has to be made of a special material.

There are two types of sterilizer available to the hobbyist (Figure 26). The

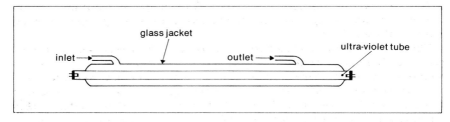

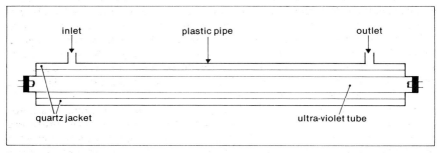

Figure 26. a) A simple ultra-violet light sterilizer. b) A quartz-jacketed sterilizer.

simplest type consists of an ultra-violet tube surrounded by a glass jacket with a centimetre or so (about ¼ in) gap between the two. The glass jacket is fitted with inlet and outlet pipes so that water can be pumped around the ultra-violet tube and back into the aquarium, having been sterilized in the process.

The advantage of this type of unit is that it is comparatively cheap. The disadvantage is that the jacket is sometimes an integral part of the tube and has to be replaced with it, which can be rather expensive. Another disadvantage is that ultra-violet tubes run much more efficiently if they are allowed to run hot. In the device mentioned, the water flowing over the tube tends to cool it and thus reduces its efficiency.

The other type of sterilizer is designed to run hot and can have up to twice the output of the cool-running type. This is achieved by surrounding the ultra-violet tube with a special quartz jacket allowing an air gap between the two. The whole assembly is then enclosed in a further plastic jacket fitted with the inlet and outlet pipes.

Quartz glass has the special property of allowing short-wave ultra-violet light to pass through it. Water is pumped between the quartz tube and the plastic jacket and is there irradiated. The tube runs hot because of the air gap separating it from the water.

This type of sterilizer has the advantages of being up to twice as efficient as the other type and having replacement tubes that are comparatively cheap. The disadvantage is that quartz glass is expensive and so the initial cost is high.

Either type has to be used in conjunction with a water pump so that water can be circulated around the unit. This can be an internal or external pump or even the outlet of a power filter.

The output of ultra-violet sterilizers is measured in microwatt seconds/cm² of tube at a given flow rate. Most sterilizers quote a flow rate that will enable the sterilizer to produce 35 000 microwatt seconds/cm², sufficient to kill off most bacteria and viruses. A 30 watt quartz jacket sterilizer will produce this amount of radiation at a flow rate of 810 l (180 gallons) per hour. A 15 watt quartz jacket sterilizer will produce the same amount of radiation at half the flow rate, 405 l (90 gallons) per hour. Sterilizers that allow water to run over the ultra-violet tube can accept as little as half the above flow rates to achieve the same amount of radiation.

The output of the sterilizer is inversely proportional to the flow rate through it. As we have seen, a 30 watt quartz sterilizer will give 35 000 microwatt seconds/cm² at a flow rate of 180 l an hour. If the flow of water is halved, the amount of radiation is doubled. If the flow rate is doubled, the radiation is halved. This principle enables a sterilizer to be sized precisely.

35 000 microwatt seconds/hour is sufficient to kill off most infectious organisms, including the troublesome marine dinoflagellate, *Oodinium ocellatum*, otherwise known as velvet or coral fish disease. Fungal infections need two or three times the power to destroy the spores. White spot disease, *Cryptocaryon irritans*, requires a far higher level of radiation to destroy it because it is a much larger organism. 800 000-1 000 000 microwatt seconds/cm² are needed, 23 times the power needed for *Oodinium*. Still larger organisms, such as flukes and lice, require such a huge amount of radiation as to make it almost impossible to destroy them by this method.

The efficacy of a sterilizer is dependent upon the clarity of the water entering it and how clean the tube is. Any particulate waste or turbidity in the water can shield disease organisms from radiation. Yellowing of the water absorbs the radiation before it can kill disease organisms.

Aquariums using a sterilizer should have good mechanical filtration to remove particulate waste, and carbon or ozone should be used to remove any yellowing. Probably the best way of using a sterilizer is to connect it to the outlet of a power filter so that only clean, freshly filtered water passes over the ultra-violet tube.

Eventually some debris will accumulate in the sterilizer and the output will be reduced. The unit should be dismantled and cleaned every couple of months to ensure optimum performance.

Ultra-violet lamps do not burn out like ordinary fluorescent tubes. Instead there is a steady decline in output with use. There is no visible indication of decreased performance because the short-wave light is invisible to the human eye, all we can see is a slight blue glow, generated by a few stray longer wavelengths. An ultra-violet tube decreases in output by about 20% to 50% per year of continuous use. If the unit is not used continuously then a record must be kept of the hours used and the tube replaced when it has had the equivalent of 1 years' use, or 6 months use if the output is critical.

There are two things to consider when calculating the flow rate and power needed in any given aquarium. Firstly, the amount of power needed to kill a particulate organism and, secondly, a turnover sufficient to destroy the organism faster than it can multiply and become contagious. The first point is easy and can be calculated with precision. The second is more difficult.

Obviously the higher the turnover, the better the chance of eradicating a disease. At the standard irradiation level of 35 000 microwatt seconds/cm^2, even small sterilizers will give quite high turnovers. For example, in a 450 l (100 gallon) aquarium, a 15 watt quartz jacket sterilizer is capable of a turnover almost equal to the volume of the tank each hour. It is generally accepted that a volume of water has to be turned over five times in order to guarantee that every drop passes through the sterilizer at least once. Even taking this into consideration, the longest time a disease organism could remain in the aquarium would be 5 hours and most would be destroyed well before this time. This is almost certainly sufficient to prevent diseases such as *Oodinium* from reaching epidemic proportions.

What about white spot disease? The large size of the organism involved means that a far higher level of radiation is needed. To use the same turnover as before would need ten 30 watt quartz-jacket sterilizers in series. This is both impractical and prohibitively expensive. If the turnover were halved, then only five units would be required which is still very expensive. Reducing the turnover to one-tenth would mean that one 30 watt sterilizer could turn over 40 l (9 gallons) per hour. Unfortunately, this would mean that a white spot organism could stay within the system for 2 days before being destroyed. This is almost certainly too slow to prevent the disease spreading.

Is a sterilizer worthwhile? It depends on what you expect from it. A sterilizer is not a universal cure and at best can only destroy free-swimming organisms. Unlike medication, it cannot kill off any disease organisms attached to the fish, so the tank must be sterilized until the organisms either drop off the fish or die of old age. Most diseases have maximum cycles of 14 days so perhaps the most economical way of using a sterilizer is to switch it on for 3 weeks each time a new fish is introduced, or when there is the slightest suspicion of disease. Do remember to find out the cost of replacement tubes when buying a sterilizer. A quartz-jacket sterilizer is initially more expensive but is probably cheaper in the long run.

Apart from intended use, there is now some evidence to suggest that a sterilizer that is run for 24 hours a day may be able to prevent the toxic tank syndrome. This is due to the fact that ultra-violet light flocculates troublesome protein molecules until they form flakes that can be filtered out. This will be discussed in Chapter 7.

Oodinium is the most troublesome disease in the marine aquarium because it is difficult to cure, even with copper-based medication. A sterilizer will prevent the disease getting out of control if used properly. On the other hand, white spot disease is difficult to destroy by sterilization because of the size of the organism. It can, however, be very easily cured by copper treatment. A sterilizer can be a useful addition to a marine system, but in a mixed invertebrate and fish tank it cannot be relied upon to control white spot and the tank cannot be treated with copper without destroying the invertebrates. Only the very brave or very foolish attempt a mixed tank, even with a sterilizer!

7

THE TOXIC TANK SYNDROME

By now you are probably bewildered and confused by the massive range of equipment available. There is a minimum amount of equipment that is essential of course; otherwise, like most other hobbies, you can spend as little or as much as you like. Generally speaking, the more you spend the better the equipment and the easier it becomes to keep even delicate creatures. However, it need not cost the earth. A simple set-up will make it possible to keep most forms of life provided that things are done slowly, carefully and patiently.

Probably the simplest and cheapest set-up involves under-gravel filters with a layer of sand on top. Providing there is adequate lighting, this system will support most of the hardier invertebrates. Unfortunately, it cannot be relied upon to keep fish in good health for any length of time. Why? The dreaded wipe-out. The American author, Martin A. Moe Jnr coined the phrase the 'toxic tank syndrome', which as we shall see, sums up an unpleasant sequence of events very well.

For years, people have been trying to keep marines with just under-gravel filters or even trickle filters. Whilst many succeeded with these systems, an equal number failed. One day they had a tank full of healthy fish, the next day a tank full of dead fish with no apparent decline in water quality. The syndrome is now understood, although the exact nature of its cause is still a matter of some debate. One thing is certain though; it can be avoided!

What is this syndrome? A tank can be set up for months, sometimes even years, and suddenly disaster will strike. I have spent much time researching this phenomenon and I have witnessed it many times. On days previous to the wipe-out, the fish behave in an odd manner as if they are diseased in some way. They hide away nervously, breathe erratically and dart wildly around the tank, sometimes scratching their gill plates. The novice usually mistakes this for an *Oodinium* or gill fluke infection and treats the tank with medication. Unfortunately, this inevitably makes thing worse. The next sign, which sometimes, but not always, appears, is an increase in foaming on the water surface. Finally most fish die over a period of a few hours in the middle of the night, although some may survive for a few days. The syndrome does not effect cleaner wrasse or related species, nor does it appear in predominantly invertebrate set-ups.

One very stange effect of this disastrous chain of events is the 'goldfish bowl' effect. This involves removing a sample of water from the toxic tank and placing it in another container, e.g. a goldfish bowl. This container can be floated inside the original tank. A fish should be placed in this bowl and another in the toxic tank. Within a few hours the fish in the toxic tank will be dead but the one in the bowl will be quite happy. Curiouser and curiouser! Once a tank has turned toxic, it is almost impossible to re-establish it. Large water changes and leaving it uninhabited for weeks seem to make no difference. At one time the only answer was to strip down the tank and start again. Wiser marine aquarists would run two tanks so that fish could be transferred to the other in the event of trouble.

The most probable cause of the problem is the bacterial toxins generated by bacteria in the filter bed or on the walls of the tank. There is some evidence to suggest that certain bacteria produce toxins as a by-product of their metabolism. These bacteria are responsible for breaking down the intermediate stages between waste products and ammonia in the nitrogen cycle. Proteins seem to be the most dangerous in this respect. In a completely stable environment, where bacteria have a constant supply of food and there are no sudden shifts in water quality, these bacteria do not normally pose a threat. Unfortunately, conditions in the aquarium are not that stable and, sooner or later, a slight imbalance may occur, leading to a rise in protein and organic waste. Perhaps the syndrome is triggered by variations in specific gravity. In any case the normally harmless bacteria produce large quantities of toxic products that now poison the tank. Once this has happened, it is very difficult to re-establish the correct balance.

Not everyone is agreed on the cause of the wipe-out. Some authorities suggest that the cause is, in fact, toxins produced by algae. Certain algae have been observed to produce massive quantities of free-swimming spores under certain conditions and these are almost certainly toxic. During mass swarming of algal spores, the tank can become slightly cloudy or discoloured. I have observed many wipe-outs where there has been absolutely no discoloration and no signs of algae when water was viewed under a microscope. Whilst algal toxins certainly exist, I believe the most common cause is the toxins generated in the filter bed by bacteria. Removing the fish to another container, such as a goldfish bowl, isolates them from the toxic filter bed. This is purely speculative and further research will probably give us the answer one day.

If the cause is a matter for some debate, the prevention of the syndrome is known with certainty. An adequate protein skimmer will almost certainly prevent the toxic tank syndrome. It is probable that skimming removes much of the organic waste and protein from the system before the bacteria can act on it. Of course, this has other benefits because the biological filter has less to cope with and so there is a slower rise in nitrate and a slower decline in pH. I would not dream of running a system without a skimmer myself.

Ozone also seems to prevent the wipe-out. This is probably because of its ability to oxidize organic waste and, like the skimmer, remove the protein before bacteria can act on it. As an ozonizer is usually used in conjunction with a protein skimmer, it should be considered of secondary importance; however, a skimmer and ozonizer run together are of considerable benefit to most systems.

Ultra-violet sterilization also seems to reduce the likelihood of trouble. Ultra-violet light has the ability to flocculate or denature proteins and probably this prevents bacteria from acting on them.

If the cause of the problem is algal toxins, then we must assume that the devices mentioned are equally efficient at removing or destroying algal spores. Protein skimming can achieve this by froth flotation, ozone by oxidizing the cells and ultra-violet light by killing the spores. So, whatever the cause, it is easily prevented.

Coming back to which system to choose, it would seem that the simplest and cheapest viable system comprises under-gravel filters, driven by an air pump, and an adequate protein skimmer.

A more elaborate system can be bought right from the start, but it is possible to upgrade the simple system described in stages, as and when extras can be afforded (Figure 27). Probably the best improvement to make initially is to add a power filter. This will help to prevent the filter under gravel from clogging up and will also enable the use of other media such as activated carbon. The more powerful the power filter, the cleaner the tank will stay. The larger the filter canister, the less often it will need cleaning. The next step would be to use water pumps to power the under-gravel filter. The main benefit here is to your ears! Air pumps do make a noise whereas water pumps are virtually silent.

An ozonizer could be fitted to pump ozone through the protein skimmer. Some skimmers have the provision for a power filter to be attached to the outlet pipe. Used in this way, water would first be skimmed and the bulk of the waste would be removed or oxidized by the ozone. Any waste remaining would then be sieved out by the power filter or absorbed by the activated carbon inside it. Carbon will also remove any traces of ozone from the water before it is returned to the tank.

Figure 27. The combined system. It is possible to start with just the basic under-gravel filter and protein skimmer. Additional equipment can be added in stages.

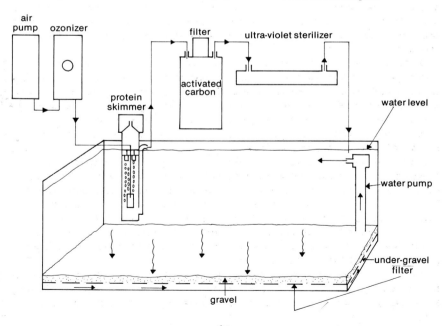

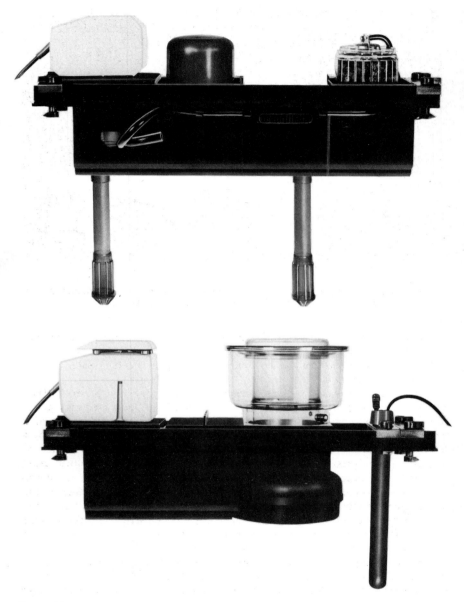

Figure 28. A complete Tunze system for sea-water use. (Above) high-power water pump, mechanical filter, osmolator, bioreactor. (Below) protein skimmer.

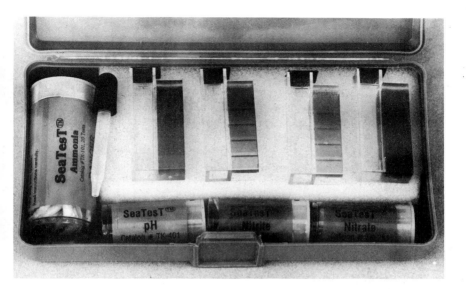

Figure 29. Accurate testing is essential. This boxed set of SeaTest kits, manufactured by Aquarium Systems, includes kits for ammonia, nitrite, nitrate and pH.

Finally an ultra-violet sterilizer could be fitted to the outlet of the power filter to kill off any bugs that manage to get through the rest of the system.

Of course, you do not have to have all this equipment. As I have said, you can spend as little or as much as you like.

If you want a really good system right from the start, then it is better to buy a ready-made *systemfilter*. The Tunze system (Figure 28) is widely used throughout Europe. The first stage of this system is a power-driven protein skimmer which removes up to 80% of organic waste. Next is a powerful water pump, run by a device called a power timer. This pulses the flow of water from the pump to provide waves of pressure rather than a steady flow. This not only eliminates dead spots within the tank, but also benefits corals and anemones by subjecting them to a swaying motion which they would experience in nature. Other features of the power timer are a food-timer button, which turns off the pump for 5 to 15 minutes while the fish and invertebrates have their food, and a photocell that reduces the power of the pump at night. This feature enables the inhabitants to rest at night without being blown around the tank by the pump.

The water pump drives a power-filter cartridge that is constructed in such a way that a fresh layer of filter material is available at all times. When the cartridge is dirty it is simply unplugged and cleaned or replaced. A carbon cartridge is also available.

The next stage, also powered by the pump, is called an osmolator. This provides a surface skimmer to remove any scum from the water surface. Inside the osmolator is a very sensitive float-switch mechanism connected to an electronically-controlled dosing pump. This automatically replaces evaporated water and keeps conditions very stable.

Finally a series of bio-reactors complete the system. These consist of trickle-filter cartridges suspended above the water surface with a submerged compartment underneath. The trickle cartridges break down ammonia to nitrate and nitrate is reduced to free nitrogen by bacteria colonizing the granular medium in the submerged compartment. Nitrate may still accumulate in heavily stocked fish systems, but, in mostly invertebrate tanks, it is possible to have virtually no nitrate. The system can be complemented with a range of electronic pH meters, electroconductivity meters and redox-potential meters.

Whatever the system you choose, it must be backed up by accurate, easy to use test kits. Remember, an inaccurate test kit will give misleading results and this is worse than having no test kit at all. Good-quality test kits are more expensive than cheap ones but will pay for themselves in the long run. The SeaTest range (Figure 29), produced by Aquarium Systems, are good quality test kits and similar to those used in laboratories. Other brands may be equally suitable, but, like most things, you get what you pay for.

8

SETTING UP YOUR AQUARIUM

This is what you have been waiting for! At last it's time to start your system running. Having got the aquarium in its permanent position, the equipment can now be added.

If under-gravel filters are to be used, then these will have to be installed first (Figure 30). The bottom of the tank must be clean and free from any specks of grit that could lodge under the edge of the filter plate. The filter plate or plates, together with their uplift tubes, can now be carefully positioned and weighted down with a couple of bricks; this will ensure that they do not move when sand is added. If you have decided on two layers of substrate then these should be added one at a time. Carefully pour the first layer over the filter bed and *very* carefully remove the bricks. Now install the plastic separating mesh; it will probably need to be weighted down with the bricks to stop it curling up. Finally the top layer of sand is poured on and the bricks are removed once more. If you are using just one

Figure 30. An under-gravel filter set up with two layers of substrate separated by a plastic mesh.

substrate, then simply pour this over the plates and remove the bricks. Of course, you may be using a method of filtration that eliminates under-gravel filters. In this case, a sprinkling of roughly 1 cm (½ in) of coral sand or gravel should be added to cover the bottom of the tank.

Now the tank is beginning to look a bit more promising! If a submerged type of protein skimmer is to be used, then this should be added at this stage so that it can later be hidden with rock work. A length of air line should be added ready to connect up to the air pump, as it may prove difficult connecting up the skimmer at a later stage.

Now some decoration may be added. Tufa rock is ideal because of its buffering capacity. Any dead corals should first be bleached for 24 hours in a solution of non-detergent bleach to remove any remaining organic debris. The bleach should be thoroughly hosed off before the corals are added to the tank. A very slight smell of bleach may persist, but this is acceptable. Dead sea fans and sea whips should not be used unless they have been treated with a special coating, otherwise, in time, they will simply fall to bits. Also available is a man-made inert material known as 'hyper-baked clay', also known by various trade names. This looks a little like living rock but it is considerably cheaper than the real thing. If you intend keeping invertebrates, then you may wish to use real living rock. Obviously this cannot be added until the tank is running, but it is possible to put in position a row of stones along the back of the tank on which the living rock can eventually be placed.

When decorating the aquarium, try not to arrange things too formally. The easiest way to achieve a natural-looking environment, even if you are not very artistic, is to simply buy pieces of rock and coral that appeal to you and select them at random when placing them in the tank. It is possible to build a large backdrop of rock and coral by using mostly thin, flat pieces built up on each other. You may prefer to have just a few pieces scattered around the bottom, as this leaves more swimming space for fish. If the set-up is to be seen from both sides, then about the only way of decorating the tank is to build up a small ridge running centrally from one end to the other, with perhaps an odd piece of coral resting on the bottom here and there.

Having decorated the tank at least partly, the next stage is to position the heater thermostats and wire them up to the electrical console. They must NOT be turned on until the water is added! The air or water pumps can now be installed and wired in.

At last it is time to add the water! Position a plate or saucer in the centre of the tank and direct a hose pipe at it, or pour buckets of water over it. The plate will prevent the coral sand bed from being disturbed. As the tank is being filled up the approximate quantity of salt may be added. You will end up with a cloudy mess, but do not worry; the pumps and heaters can now be switched on.

The water has to be left now for 48 hours before the specific gravity can be checked. The intervening time can be spent wiring up the lights and power filters if they are to be used. Note that activated carbon or ozone should not be used in new sea water as there is a danger of altering the chemistry, due to the fact that there is not yet much in the way of organic waste.

When the tank is up to temperature and the water is fairly clean, the specific gravity can be checked and adjusted if necessary. Now the biological filter has to be matured.

If possible, seed the tank with dirty coral sand from an established system. Simply take a handful or two of sand and sprinkle it over the bottom of the tank; this applies even if under-gravel filters are not being used. This will introduce all the friendly bacteria that keep the water pure and healthy. If this is not possible then do not be concerned, the bacteria will find their own way into the tank but it will just take a while longer to mature. The next stage is to introduce a source of organic waste and ammonia. In a fish-only system, this can be achieved either by introducing one or two hardy fish or by using a commercial brand of quick-. maturing agent. The result will be the same either way, except that with the fish method, the tank may take 2 or 3 months to mature whereas, with the chemical method, it usually takes only 3 to 6 weeks.

Either way, once nutrients have been added to the water, the bacteria will start to multiply. In the first stage, a steady rise in ammonia occurs and this can be monitored with an ammonia test kit, although this is not essential. Soon bacteria will break down the ammonia to nitrite and, at this point, you will get a steady rise in nitrite which should be monitored with a test kit. Nitrite will continue to rise because ammonia inhibits the bacteria that normally break down nitrite to nitrate. The nitrite level will normally peak somewhere between 5 and 15 p.p.m., depending on the type of filter being used. At about this stage, all the ammonia has been used up and so the bacteria that act on nitrite are no longer inhibited. This causes a rapid drop in nitrite, as now it can be broken down to nitrate, the usual end-product. The whole process can easily be monitored by checking the nitrite level every few days. Over a period of weeks, the nitrite level will steadily climb and then, quite suddenly, it will collapse, indicating that the filter is now mature.

With an invertebrate tank, living rock can be used to mature the tank. Living rock harbours so many bacteria and organisms that it is capable of maturing a tank on its own. A few pieces should be selected from a dealer's tank. They should have been in stock for at least a week so that any decomposition of organisms killed during transport will take place in the dealer's tank, not yours. The rock should be positioned in the tank so that only the minimum possible amount is actually touching the sand. Living rock needs water to circulate around it to keep it alive. Where it is in contact with the sand, most of the organisms will die and the rock will turn white. The nitrite level should be closely monitored. It may rise and fall or, if you are lucky, it may not appear at all. When there has been no nitrite reading for a week, one or two hardy organisms can be added and the nitrite checked again. Living rock should not be used to mature a fish-only tank because any future copper treatment will kill it.

Although the nitrite may disappear after a few weeks, it must be remembered that the system actually takes 6 to 9 months to become completely stable, so it is important not to add anything too delicate during this period.

It is quite usual for the pH to drop dramatically when the tank matures. This is due to the massive level of bacterial activity as they multiply to cope with the load.

It is not necessary to correct the pH until the tank is actually mature. The best thing is to make a 50% water change before adding livestock. Leave things to settle down for a few days and, if necessary, add a buffer to the water. Providing that the pH is above 8.0 things are going all right. Attempts to raise the pH higher should be left until the system is more stable.

It is quite normal to have a brown dusty film over everything within the tank. This is caused by minute creatures called diatoms. Given enough light it should eventually be superseded by a growth of green algae. In a fish-only tank that is not brightly lit the film may die back but some will always remain. It is quite harmless.

9

YOUR FIRST FISH

So now you are ready to buy your first fish or invertebrate. Before deciding *what* to buy, give some thought as to *where* you buy. If you only have one dealer nearby then the choice is easy, but if you have several shops within an hour's drive you should visit them all before deciding. Choose a quiet day, visit a shop and have a word with the dealer. The first thing to decide is whether he really knows what he is talking about! As a beginner, you may be forgiven for automatically assuming that anyone who sells marines must know all about them. Marine fish keeping is a very technical subject and it is a sad fact that some dealers simply do not have sufficient knowledge. After you have kept marines for some years you may well find that it is often the case that the customer knows more than the dealer! Old established dealers may give good advice but may have a rather old-fashioned outlook. Years ago they found a way of keeping marines and have stuck with it ever since. This type of dealer invariably shuns new technology and may not be up-to-date with the latest breakthroughs.

CHOICE OF DEALER

Shop around and pick out a few shops that are up to date and whose staff seem to know what they are talking about. They will all give conflicting advice on which is the best system to buy. Doubtless many will disagree with what I have written in this book! Not to worry, different people find different things work for them. They are probably all quite correct in what they say, but it can be confusing hearing so much different advice. This is the first reason for picking out one dealer and staying with him. At least the advice will be consistent.

What about the fish? Does your dealer have a good turnover of livestock, or is he just losing fish and replacing them? A good shop should either quarantine fish for 2 weeks before sale or, at least, advise you that a particular fish has not been in stock for very long. Fish invariably carry some disease or parasite when newly imported and it is preferable for your dealer to be faced with the problem rather than you. Beware of shops offering fish for sale very cheaply. The specimens are probably unquarantined and sold as soon as they are imported; this minimizes the dealer's losses and keeps prices low. They may be fish that have been caught illegally. It is a sad fact that, in some countries, the environment and everything in it is being destroyed by fish-exporters catching fish with cyanide and explosives. These fish are offered for sale cheaply but are lucky to live for more than a few weeks.

Choose a dealer who really takes a personal interest in his fish. He should be able to tell you how long the fish has been in the shop and what it feeds on. Do not be

Figure 31. Black pyramid butterfly (*Hemitaurichthys zoster*). Many butterflies are delicate fish and are usually finicky feeders. This one is an exception to the rule, being hardy and eating most foods. Unfortunately, it is seldom imported.

frightened to ask to see a fish feeding. If the dealer has nothing to hide, he should willingly oblige.

A healthy fish should feed well and should show no signs of wasting. Look for a nice plump specimen, not one that is pinched above the eyes. Some fish may hide away in a corner; this may be because they are unwell, do not like their tank mates or simply do not like people looking at them! Even if a fish is shy, it should still come and feed.

So now you have a dealer that has sound knowledge and time to share it with you, *and* a good varied stock of healthy fish kept in clean aquariums. Now for the second reason for staying loyal to one shop. If you have problems with your marine aquarium, the dealer should help you. If you have bought all your equipment and fish from him, he should have some knowledge of your set-up and know the fish you have bought. If you have bought from other shops as well, then he cannot be responsible for any disease that may have come from elsewhere. If, having spent your money, you are dissatisfied, then by all means change and explain the situation to your new supplier.

Even the best dealers are usually unwilling to give any guarantee with livestock. Put yourself in the dealer's position. You buy a fish that has lived happily in his tank for weeks, you take it home and it dies. Of course you may have bought a sick fish but the dealer has no way of knowing whether the fish was unfit or whether you murdered it! If you do lose fish, then by all means mention it to the shop. They may have had problems with a particular batch of fish themselves, in which case they may be willing to replace it. At worst your dealer can offer advice on what may have gone wrong. Treat your dealer with some respect and in turn your dealer should treat you well.

CHOICE OF FISH

So what fish should you start with? The best bet is to buy one or two very hardy fish to try out the system. If the tank is not completely mature there will be a rise in ammonia and nitrite. It is therefore important to purchase initially fish that are tolerant of poor conditions; these are known as *nitrite-tolerant fish*. Probably the most indestructible fish are those that can live in fresh or salt water, these are known as *brackish-water fish*.

Brackish-water fish

Monodactylus argenteus (mono, fingerfish, Malayan angel, Singapore angel, silver moonfish, silver leaf fish): A lively fish, fairly peaceful. Seldom exceeds 15 cm (6 in).

Poecilia spheops (black molly): Friendly, peaceful fish. Should not be kept with aggressive species. Grows to 7 cm (3 in).

Scatophagus argus (scat): A rather greedy boisterous fish, tending to be a little aggressive. Should not be kept with anything too delicate. Seldom exceeds 15 cm (6 in).

Nitrite-tolerant fish (living only in sea water)

Damselfish
Abudefduf cyaneus (electric blue damsel, Fiji devil, blue reef fish): Small reasonably peaceful fish. Does better in a shoal. Up to 4 cm (1 ½ in).

Abudefduf oxyodon (blue velvet damselfish): A pretty but aggressive and territorial fish. Must be kept with larger fish or will nip fins. Grows to 8 cm (3 in).

Abudefduf saxatilis (sergeant major): Very similar to *A. sexfasciatus*. Individual specimens can be spiteful. Grows to a maximum of 12 cm (5 in).

Abudefduf xanthurus (orange-tailed devil): Very aggressive. Grows to 15 cm (6 in).

Chromis spp.: Attractive and peaceful damsels. Rather delicate and best kept in a shoal. Not recommended for a new tank.

Dascyllus aibisella (one-spot domino): Fairly aggressive but all right with other hardy fish. Seldom exceeds 7 cm (3 in).

Dascyllus aruanus (white-tailed damselfish, three-striped humbug): Rather territorial. Has been known to pull hairs off aquarists' arms in defence of its territory! Up to 7 cm (3 in).

Dascyllus melanurus (black-tailed damselfish, four-striped humbug): Not quite as spiteful as *D. aruanus* but otherwise similar.

Dascyllus trimaculatus (three-spot domino): Similar to *D. aibisella*.

Eupomacentrus fuscus (dusky damselfish, black damselfish): Extremely hardy but fairly aggressive. Seldom exceeds 10 cm (4 in).

Eupomacentrus leucostictus (beau Gregory): One of the most beautiful of the damsels when small but colour fades in large specimens. Grows to a maximum of 15 cm (6 in).

Clownfish

These fish are very popular and interesting due to their well known symbiotic relationship with anemones. A clownfish wallowing in its 'feather-bed' of tentacles is an intriguing sight.

Amphiprion akallopisos (skunk clown, orange skunk): Spiteful to any new fish introduced. Will even attack fish five times its own size. Small specimens are more peaceful. Up to 5 cm (2 in).

Amphiprion biaculeatus (maroon clown, spiny-cheeked clown): Very hardy but very territorial and aggressive. Will not usually tolerate another clownfish in its tank but is all right with fish of dissimilar markings. Up to 9 cm (4 in).

Amphiprion clarkii (yellow-tailed clown): A particularly handsome fish. Fairly peaceful towards other fish but often spiteful to its own kind. Addition of more anemones may prevent fighting. Up to 10 cm (4 in).

Amphiprion ephippium (tomato clown, fire clown): Peaceful when small. May bully smaller fish and other clowns when large. Up to 8 cm (3 in).

Amphiprion frenatus (red clown, tomato clown, fire clown): Very similar to and often confused with *A. ephippium*.

Amphiprion percula (percula clown, common clown): Attractive and peaceful fish. Will only attack other clowns added at a later date. This species is very prone to clownfish disease, particularly specimens from Singapore. It is important to check that the fish has been in stock for at least 3 weeks before purchase.

Amphiprion perideraion (pink skunk clown): Similar to *A. akalopisos.*

Amphiprion polymnus (saddle-backed clown): Rather sensitive to nitrite and is not suitable for a new tank.

Amphiprion sebae (brown and white clown): Very peaceful. Grows to 9 cm (4 in) maximum.

Triggerfish
Very hardy fish, triggers have a good set of teeth and a razor-sharp trigger near the dorsal (back) fin. Some species can be downright vicious, so care should be taken when handling.

Balistapus undulatus (undulate trigger): A real character. Will pick up large

Figure 32. Ringens trigger (*Melichthys ringens*). Triggers are exceptionally hardy but some species, including this one, can be aggressive, particularly to newcomers.

chunks of coral and rock and redecorate the tank to its own liking. Vicious. Grows to 25 cm (10 in).

Balistes bursa (bursa trigger): Aggressive to its own kind but suitable to put with large hardy fish. Up to 18 cm (7 in). (See also *Rhineacanthus.*)

Balistes vetula (queen trigger): Pretty but dangerous! Up to 25 cm (10 in).

Balistoides niger (clown trigger, conspicuous trigger): One of the most spectacular and sought after marine fish. Very unpredictable. Sometimes peaceful with existing fish, even small ones, but will often attack newcomers. Will sometimes attack fingers! Commands a high price. Grows slowly to 20 cm (8 in) in captivity but can reach 60 cm (24 in) in the wild.

Melichthys ringens (black-finned trigger, Figure 32): Of similar temperament to *B. niger*.

Melichthys vidua (pink-tailed trigger): One of the exceptions to the triggers. Very peaceful and friendly fish with a personality. Grows to 25 cm (10 in) in a large tank. Watch your fingers when feeding it!

Odonus niger (Black trigger, blue trigger): Similar to *M. vidua* in temperament but rather shy. Should not be kept with anything too aggressive.

Rhinecanthus aculeatus and *R. rectangulus* (humu-huhu-nuku-nuku-a-puaa): both these fish are similar in appearance and temperament to *Balistes bursa*. Aggressive to their own species but suitable with larger hardy fish. Up to 18 cm (7 in).

Filefish

These are somewhat similar to triggers but are rather more delicate and should not be put in a new tank.

Eels

Echidna spp. and *Gymnothorax* spp.: These are all various types of moray eel. Morays are almost indestructible and quite peaceful except that anything that will fit in their mouths is considered as fair game. May need tempting with food on the end of a knitting needle. Can give a nasty nip if you are over-enthusiastic at feeding time. Grows to 1 m (about 3 ft).

Batfish

Platax orbicularis (orbiculate batfish): A popular fish when small, it often outgrows its welcome. Being a greedy fish, it grows rapidly to 50 cm (18 in), even in a small aquarium and loses its attractive colour when large. An interesting character fish nevertheless.

Platax pinnatus: A startlingly beautiful batfish but extremely difficult to feed. Not suitable for the beginner.

Platax teira (long-finned batfish): Slower-growing but more attractive than *P. orbicularis*. Its long fins make it a target for fin nippers so it should only be kept with peaceful fish. Grows as large as *P. orbicularis* but more slowly.

Lionfish
These are spectacular and popular but it must be noted that the dorsal spines are venomous. I once had the misfortune to be stung by one of these and I can verify that it is an excruciatingly painful experience. These fish are not normally bad-tempered but must be treated with respect. They will eat any fish small enough to swallow but are otherwise peaceful. They can be very difficult to feed on anything other than live food. A good idea is to thread some live food onto a piece of cotton and bob it up and down in front of the fish's nose. This almost always triggers off the feeding response.

Pterois volitans (volitans lionfish, turkeyfish, scorpion fish, butterfly cod): This is the least finnicky of the lionfish to feed and is the only one recommended to the beginner. Grows fairly rapidly to 26 cm (10 in).

Rabbitfish
These are not often imported because of their rather dull colouration. They have poisonous dorsal fins that can give a painful sting. Can change colour at will with startling results!

Siganus corallinus (spotted rabbitfish) and *Siganus vermiculatus* (vermiculated rabbitfish): Friendly, hardy and peaceful fish and usually good 'characters'. Excellent for eating algae. Grow to 15 cm (6 in).

Lo vulpinus (fox-face, badger fish, rabbitfish): exceptionally for a rabbitfish, this species is a beautiful vivid yellow. An excellent fish for any aquarium.

Unless otherwise stated any of these fish are suitable in a new aquarium because if anything is not quite right, they should tolerate the adverse conditions. When buying your first fish do not rush into a decision. Do think firstly of what other fish you ultimately hope to keep and make sure that your first purchase will be compatible. For example a Clown Trigger is a fine fish but you may be disappointed to find that it kills any other fish you try to introduce.

If the aquarium is an invertebrate tank then living rock will be the first thing to put in. To play on the safe side, only nitrite tolerant invertebrates should be added for the first few weeks. These include cleaner shrimps, dancing shrimps, boxing shrimps, sea cucumbers, fan worms, *Radianthus* species, anemones, crabs, lobsters and most prawns. Starfish, sea urchins, live corals, gorgonians and some species of anemone are notably intolerant of poor conditions and should not be added to a new tank.

10
ROUTINE MAINTENANCE

Contrary to popular belief, a marine aquarium does not require much attention once things have settled down. The first thing for the beginner to learn is not to overfeed. This is particularly important in a new tank because the biological filter will not have developed its maximum potential and can be easily overloaded. Feed your pets sparingly. Fish should eat all available food within a few minutes. Invertebrates may take longer, particularly grazers, such as sea cucumbers. If uneaten food is evident after an hour or so, then the inhabitants have been overfed and excess food must be removed. This is easily done by siphoning with a length of hose or by using a purpose-built aquarium vacuum-cleaner.

A frequent problem in a new set-up is pH. The massive increase in bacterial activity often has the effect of keeping pH rather low. Hardy creatures, recommended in the previous chapter, will tolerate low pH for some time. More delicate creatures are not so tolerant and the pH must be kept at a minimum of 8.1. Initially, it may be necessary to change 25% of the water each week. After this period, small additions of sodium bicarbonate or a commercial brand of buffer should do the trick. If the pH reading remains high in a new tank then you have probably got an inaccurate test kit! For some odd reason, cheap test kits tend to overread the pH reading, some by as much as 0.3 units. This is an error big enough to be a matter of life and death to the inhabitants of your aquarium.

If you can afford it, an electronic pH meter is well worth while and saves much wasted time and uncertainty. If you are in any doubt about the accuracy of a chemical test kit, it may be possible to compare the results with an electronic meter. Failing this, it may be possible to obtain pH buffering powders used to calibrate electronic meters. These mix with distilled water to give a solution of a known pH. It does not matter too much if your test kit does overread, providing you know by how much. It is then a simple matter to take this into consideration when taking readings.

Evaporated water needs replacing at least weekly. Because of the warmth of the aquarium water, a lot of fresh water is lost through evaporation, particularly in situations where there are no condensation trays. It is a simple matter to replace this water with tap water; such small amounts are involved that it is not necessary to treat the tap water before use.

The more often the tank is topped up the better. Delicate invertebrates and seaweeds cannot adjust to a constantly changing density and will soon die if bucketfuls of fresh water are sloshed into the tank every few weeks. Once again, technology comes to the rescue. There is now available a device (an osmolator, see p. 65) which automatically replaces evaporated water. It has a sensitivity of only 5 ml (1 teaspoonful) and is a useful addition if you can afford it.

Most marine systems utilize some type of biological filter that relies upon bacteria to digest the waste products present. Usually these products are converted to nitrate, which is harmless at low levels. As we have seen, most delicate species will tolerate up to 20 p.p.m., hardier animals up to 50 or 60 p.p.m., without any apparent ill effect. The action of most biological filters produces a steady quantity of nitrate which will continue to rise unless corrective action is taken.

Normally, changing 25% of the water each month is sufficient to keep the nitrate down to a reasonable level. This method does have its disadvantages. On the one hand, perfectly good sea water might be poured down the drain and replacing water unnecessarily may upset the osmotic balance. On the other hand, if not enough water is changed then, over the years, the nitrate level may reach several hundred p.p.m. A good, accurate nitrate test kit is invaluable. Once again, some of the cheaper tests are inaccurate and tend to under-read. If you use under-gravel filters and think you have zero nitrate after a couple of months without a water change, then the chances are that the nitrate test kit has been on the shelf too long and needs throwing in the rubbish bin. Good test kits do not deteriorate rapidly with age (within reason!).

Probably the best method of doing water changes is to keep a spare aquarium or non-toxic plastic bin full of aged sea water, ready for use. The container should be filled with tap water and, if chloramine is present, the water should be aerated for at least a week before salt is added. If the tap water is treated with ordinary chlorine then the salt can be mixed immediately, but should still be aerated for a few days before use.

Simply siphon off the appropriate amount of water from the main aquarium (siphoning off any debris that may be present at the same time) and pour it down the drain. Fill a bucket with water from the holding tank and, if necessary, take the chill off it with boiled water. (Do NOT use water from the hot tap as this contains copper.) Check the specific gravity and carefully pour it into the main tank. Not much trouble to go to once a month, is it?

At the time of writing, new biological filter systems (denitrifying systems) are becoming available that take things one stage further; nitrate is reduced to free nitrogen which is released to the atmosphere as a gas. With such systems, it is possible to maintain nitrate at very low levels, as in nature. Perhaps by the time you read this such systems will be commonplace and nitrate-producing systems will be treated with contempt!

One such denitrifying system consists of a trickle filter, containing porous biologically active granules, suspended above the water surface. Organic waste and ammonia is converted to nitrate as water is slowly trickled over the granules. Immediately beneath the trickle filter is a submerged compartment which again holds porous granules. Water passes through this chamber very slowly and nitrate is reduced to nitrogen by denitrifying bacteria that utilize the nitrate as a food source. Such a system is marketed by Tunze.

There are in fact several rather complicated technical reasons why such a system should not work. Stephen Spotte once described the art of keeping marines as 'a blend of witchcraft and science'. This is a classic example of just such a blend;

technically speaking the system should not work. In practice, it works perfectly and the nitrate will not increase, providing that the system is not heavily loaded. A strange aspect of this type of system is that it is incapable of getting rid of any nitrate that may already be in the water so, if the tap water you start with contains 20 p.p.m. of nitrate, the water in the aquarium will stay that way.

In order to keep the nitrate level close to zero with such a system, it is necessary to start with nitrate-free water. If local tap water contains nitrate then it may be necessary to use distilled or de-ionised water for the initial sea-salt mix.

The big question now is whether water changes are necessary in an aquarium with a denitrifying system. If there is no nitrate, why change the water? This question is a matter of some debate and doubtless always will be. There are those who suggest that nitrate is relatively harmless on its own but is a good indication of the build-up of other toxic compounds. There is some truth in this. Other organic compounds that cannot be broken down by a biological filter do build up and are probably more harmful than nitrate if left unchecked. The yellowing of aged aquarium water is a clear sign of this process. Fortunately this waste matter is easily removed by activated carbon so perhaps we need not be too concerned about it.

Changing water also replenishes trace elements and vitamins that have been removed by the living creatures or lost through protein skimming and carbon filtration. Again, this can easily be put right. Regular additions of trace elements and vitamins will ensure that there is no lack of these essential ingredients. In fish-only tanks, enough trace elements are supplied by way of food and such additions are normally unnecessary.

On the face of it then, it would appear that, as long as there is no nitrate, there is no need to change water. Even pH will remain constant because denitrification counter-acts the decline in pH caused by nitrification.

Personally, I would change the water even if there was no nitrate. The changes could perhaps be reduced to as little as a quarter of the normal level, say 5% per month instead of 20%. Why? After a year or so without water changes, I would imagine that the water in the aquarium would no longer resemble natural sea water very much. Some compounds may build up undetected, others may become depleted. Regular water changes probably help to keep things in balance.

Another thing that should be checked routinely is the protein skimmer. Check the collecting cup at least weekly and empty it when necessary. Water removed by the protein skimmer should be replaced with new sea water if a very stable environment is to be achieved. Usually the protein-skimmer reactor tube will need cleaning every month or so. The inside of the skimmer will become coated with cellulose and fat, which will inhibit its efficiency.

If the output of the protein skimmer decreases and a thick sludge collects instead of a liquid, it may be necessary to add a foam-inducing agent, such as Hydrokoll manufactured by HW. This will improve the efficiency of the skimmer and help to convert fat to a form that can be removed by the skimmer.

Trace element and vitamin supplements (Figure 33) are available. In a fish-only tank, it is probably unnecessary to add supplements as fish should get all they need from the food they eat. Invertebrates and algaes do absorb many substances from

Figure 33. Sea-water supplements can be useful, especially in invertebrate aquariums.

the water and these will become depleted with time, especially if protein skimming and activated carbon are used. In these circumstances, trace elements, plant foods and vitamins may be useful. As a rule of thumb, it there is a lush growth of algae then there are probably sufficient nutrients in the water.

If a power filter is used then its output should be checked frequently. When the output has dropped by about a third it is in need of a clean-out. Be careful not to destroy bacteria if a biological filter medium is used.

Where under-gravel filters are used, they should be checked every month or so. Coral sand will become compacted and clogged with debris. When doing a water change, the sand may be stirred up and the detritus siphoned off with a hose. Eventually the coral sand may dissolve to form a fine powdery material through which water cannot pass. In this case, the coral sand must be replaced. It should be done very gradually and carefully over a couple of months so as not to upset the biological balance. Remove a strip of coral sand from one end of the tank and replace it with fresh sand. The next week replace the adjoining strip of sand and so on. On no account should the filter bed be removed and cleaned or replaced; death of livestock will always follow such a drastic step!

It is often the case that algae begin to cover the inside glass of the aquarium. The easiest way of cleaning the front glass of a tank is to use a magnetic algae cleaner. This consists of two magnets; one goes on the outside of the tank and the other on the inside. The inside magnet has a plastic scouring pad attached to it which removes algae with ease. A simple device that saves a lot of swearing and wet arms!

The inside of the back of the tank, and preferably the sides as well, should be left uncleaned. If a layer of algae grows here, then so much the better. It is a valuable source of food for fish and invertebrates; remember, also, that algae can absorb many undesirable substances from the water.

Corals and rocks will be sparkling clean and white when first added to the set-up but will soon become discoloured wth algae. Unless this really bothers you, it is better to leave well alone. Tank decorations soon become covered with algae and useful nitrifying bacteria. Coral rock in particular, with its rough porous surface, harbours a substantial amount of useful organisms. If you really must clean these decorations, it is best achieved by soaking in a solution of non-detergent bleach or the hypochlorite which is used as a source of chlorine for swimming pools. Be sure to rinse well before returning to the aquarium.

Going on holiday? Lucky you! But what about your poor old fish. They will be all right for a week without food without any problem. In the wild, the often have to go without food for lengths of time. In fact, a period of fast now and then probably does them good. When you return, you will probably find that they have eaten all the algae and doubtless they will be very pleased to see you, but at least they will be alive and well.

If the holiday is for longer than a week, then it may be necessary to ask a neighbour to look after them. This is usually a potential disaster because neighbours almost always overfeed. It is probably best to make up individual food parcels, to be fed every day or two, and keep them in the freezer. All other sources of food should be hidden to avoid temptation. Whatever you do, do NOT overfeed before leaving. This can only result in uneaten food being left in the tank and this will slowly decompose and poison your tank while you are away.

It is not a bad idea to ask your neighbour to keep an eye on the thermometer and filter pumps while you are away. Do not leave reams of instructions of what to do when things go wrong but simply leave a telephone number or address at which you, or at least someone familiar with your tank, can be contacted.

There are now available automatic feeding devices. These normally consist of a hopper suitable for storing a supply of dried food and a timing mechanism that may be set to feed the fish one or more times a day. These devices are useful, particularly at holiday times, but they are limited to dried food. Most marines will survive on dried food for considerable lengths of time but they really need a more varied diet of frozen foods. Some fish will only feed on frozen food in which case an automatic feeder may not be suitable.

11

TEST KITS AND
TROUBLE-SHOOTING

If there is the slightest suspicion that something is wrong, just stop and think before reaching for the medications. If the fish look unhappy there may well be something wrong with the water quality. The symptoms of poisoning are similar to those of some diseases. If the fish are being poisoned, then adding medication will just make things worse.

If the fish are scratching, looking nervous or distressed, lying on their sides, gasping for air, trying to jump out of the tank or swimming abnormally, then check the water quality first. Even if fish are showing obvious signs of disease and are covered in spots it is still a good idea to check the water first. It may be that a decline in water quality has brought about the disease. In any case, medication should not be used unless the water quality is 100%.

Let us first check the water chemistry with a range of test kits.

WATER CHEMISTRY

Ammonia

Until recently this test kit has been rather neglected because the reagents used were unreliable and seldom gave consistent readings. This has now changed with the introduction of a new dry reagent that is very sensitive. Some test kits carry complicated tables to distinguish between ionized and un-ionized ammonia (sometimes called *ammonium* and ammonia). The relationship between the two varies with pH and temperature. Although ammonium is possibly less toxic than ammonia, this need not concern the aquarist simply because if things are working properly there should be no ammonia or ammonium at all!

Good test kits measure total ammonia, which is the total of both forms. Ammonia is measured as ammonia, or N (the N standing for nitrogen). This is just a way of simplifying measurements so that 1 unit of ammonia will give 1 unit of nitrite which, in turn, will give 1 unit of nitrate. All three compounds are measured in mg/l or p.p.m. which, to all intents and purposes, are one and the same thing.

In a mature healthy tank, ammonia should not exceed 0.1 p.p.m. After heavy feeding, this may rise temporarily to 0.2 p.p.m. If the reading is higher than this, then something if wrong. If the reading is 0.4 p.p.m. or less, the chances are that the fish will survive while the fault is rectified. Ammonia will normally subside within 3 days of corrective action being taken. If the reading is higher than this, then drastic action must be taken or the fish will probably die.

If something goes wrong, then an ammonia reading will be obtained almost immediately. The most common causes of raised ammonia levels are listed below:

a) *Immature filter*. The biological filter has not been properly matured before the introduction of livestock. In this case, the ammonia level will continue to rise and then rapidly fall. It is usually, but not always, followed by a sharp rise and eventual collapse of nitrite. If the tank has been pre-matured, it may be that insufficient bacteria are established to cope with the load. In this case, the ammonia level should fall within 5 or 6 days. Both are good reasons why an aquarium should be started off with hardy fish!

b) *Fish or invertebrates overfed*. Heavy feeding will produce more waste matter than the filter can cope with. Uneaten food will decay and produce ammonia directly. It is probably a good idea not to feed, or at least to cut down greatly on food, whilst there is ammonia or nitrite present.

c) *Biological filter damaged by excess medication*. The usual culprit here is copper. Copper is best used with a copper test kit to avoid over-dosing. A sudden dose of copper will kill off part of the filter bed. Eventually a strain of copper tolerant bacteria will take over and the ammonia level will subside. Ammonia readings of up to 0.3 p.p.m. are acceptable during copper treatment; above this, copper medication must be discontinued immediately. Ammonia levels should subside within 3 days.

d) *Biological filter damaged by poisoning*. Household chemicals can often get into an aquarium unnoticed and kill bacteria in the filter bed. Trickle filters that are suspended above the water surface are particularly susceptible to this. The usual culprits are window-cleaning fluid, fly spray, carpet shampoo and paint fumes. Excess ozone will also damage trickle filters if allowed to build up within the aquarium canopy. Ammonia levels will usually subside when the source of poisoning has been removed. If the poisoning is particularly severe, then the livestock may be harmed directly. If the poison is not biodegradable then it may be necessary to strip the tank down and start again.

e) *Power cut*. If the electricity supply has been off for more than a couple of hours, ammonia levels will rise. The waste products from the fish and invertebrates will not be broken down normally. If an under-gravel filter is used then the oxygen supply to the bacteria will be halted and anaerobic bacteria will start a process of reduction and convert nitrate back to ammonia. Trickle filters are completely unaffected as oxygen is still available to the bacteria. With under-gravel filters, power cuts of up to 12 hours are permissible in an emergency. Trickle filters will last for days without harm but the ammonia level may rise as a result of there being no filtration. The ammonia level should fall to zero within 3 days of power being re-established.

Whatever the cause of the ammonia rise, it may be necessary to take drastic action if it is too high. Large water changes will bring down the ammonia level proportionately but if it is sky-high then the inhabitants should be removed from the tank. Livestock may be transferred to a hospital or quarantine tank, or even a large bucket of sea water. It is important to remove livestock from the ammonia or it will surely die. Fish can only be left in a tank without a filter for a short time or the ammonia level will rise again. If fish are transferred to a large bucket, heavy aeration must be supplied and the ammonia level checked every few hours. It is a drastic step but may do the trick while the main tank is sorted out.

An ammonia test kit is a useful aid when keeping fish in a bare tank for reasons of quarantine or treatment with medication. The ammonia level will rise because there is no filter. A 50% water change is needed each time the ammonia level exceeds 0.4 p.p.m. It is advisable in this situation to use aged sea water from the main tank as raw freshly-mixed sea water can cause stress.

An ammonium test kit is also useful for checking tap water for chloramine.

Nitrite

A nitrite test kit is something that all marine aquarists should possess. Unlike ammonia, nitrite is very simple to test for and even cheap test kits will at least give an indication that nitrite is present.

Ammonia is converted to nitrite by nitrifying bacteria, so that it is often the case that a nitrite reading only tells you that there was previously an ammonia surge. It is possible to have ammonia present without nitrite and *vice versa*, so it is important to check for both.

Nitrite is far less toxic than ammonia. Older publications may warn that even a trace of nitrite is lethal. This popular misconception came about because, until recently, ammonia was difficult to test for. As there is usually a nitrite reading when disaster strikes a filtration system, it has been assumed in the past that nitrite was responsible for the deaths of fish. In actual fact, it is invariably ammonia that is the culprit and, providing that there is no ammonia present, most of the hardier fish will tolerate up to 4 p.p.m. of nitrite for several days with little ill effect. (N.B. Nitrite *is* toxic in fresh water!) However, only the very hardiest of fish can tolerate both ammonia and nitrite together. As this combination is always present during the maturing process, it is vital to ensure that a system is properly mature before introducing delicate fish. There should be no detectable nitrite in a mature system.

The following are the most likely causes of a nitrite reading:

a) *Immature filter*. The filter has not been properly matured before the introduction of livestock. In this case, there is first a rise and fall of ammonia followed by a rise and rapid collapse of nitrite. The maturing process can take many weeks and, for a brief period, both ammonia and nitrite exist together. Water changes will temporarily reduce the nitrite content but nature must take its course and nitrite has to peak. Reduce or stop feeding and, if possible, reduce the number of fish in the tank. Seeding the system with mature gravel can often speed things up to the extent that nitrite levels will collapse after 2 weeks.

b) *Insufficient filtration or tank overloaded*. A biological filter can only cope with so much. An overloaded filter cannot break down the waste products fast enough and there will be a constant level of ammonia. In such cases, the stocking rate must be reduced or the filter improved. With under-gravel filters, increasing the turnover may do the trick. Do not increase the turnover of trickle filters as this will only make matters worse. Trickle filters only operate properly at a certain flow rate and this must not be tampered with; instead additional trickle cartridges must be added. Nitrite should be undetectable within 3 days of corrective action being taken.

c) *Biological filter damaged by excess medication*. In this case, a positive nitrite reading indicates that there was, and perhaps still is, an ammonia reading. If nitrite is present on its own the filter is probably recovering. (See *Ammonia*, p. 84.)

d) *Unnoticed dead fish or invertebrates*. Look behind rocks and corals for rotting corpses! Nitrite levels should subside within 2 days of the culprit being removed.

e) *Biological filter damaged by poisoning*. (See *Ammonia,* p. 84.) In severe cases of poisoning, the water may become so polluted as to make it impossible to re-establish the nitrogen cycle, in which case the tank must be refilled with new water. Nitrite cannot subside until ammonia has decreased as ammonia inhibits the bacteria that use up nitrite.

f) *Power cut.* (See *Ammonia*, p. 84.)

g) *Dead spots in under-gravel filter*. Under-gravel filters gradually become clogged up and balls of debris may form blocking the flow of water. This will cause the formation of nitrite by anaerobic bacteria. The filter bed must be raked through and detritus removed.

With reverse flow under-gravel filters, the water may push its way through in just a few places, taking the easiest route. In this case, dead spots will accumulate in between. Raking through the filter bed should put matters right. This phenomena creates, in effect, small patches of quicksand in the filter bed. It may be checked for by injecting a harmless dye into the water flow to the filter plates. The dye should emerge evenly, otherwise there are dead spots present.

Nitrate

Until recently nitrate was a difficult thing to test for. Little research had been done to improve test kits because nitrate was considered to be unimportant. Recent research has indicated that high nitrate levels can cause adverse effects in the marine aquarium, especially to more delicate life forms.

Fortunately, new technology has provided us with a very simple and accurate nitrate test kit using dry reagents. Now nitrate can be monitored with ease it is a simple matter to keep levels within the limits mentioned in Chapter 10.

Nitrate levels that continue to rise rapidly and necessitate a larger than usual number of water changes are due to one of the following:

a) *Insufficient protein skimming*. A good protein skimmer is capable of removing up to 80% of available organic waste before it reaches the biological filter. As bacteria in the filter are directly responsible for the creation of nitrate, it makes sense to remove as much waste as possible before bacteria can act on it. Protein skimming can reduce the rise in nitrate to a quarter of its normal rate.

b) *Insufficient carbon filtration*. Although carbon cannot be compared with the actions of a protein skimmer, it is capable of reducing the rise in nitrate to some extent. It is an excellent medium for removing organic waste but its effects on nitrate are limited by the fact that bacteria are still able to produce nitrate from the products adsorbed onto the carbon. Nevertheless a good quality carbon can reduce the increase in nitrate to about two-thirds of its normal rate.

c) *Overstocking*. A high population of livestock produces a greater amount of waste product which in turn is converted to nitrate.

Unlike ammonia or nitrite, nitrate will not fall after corrective action has been taken. It can only accumulate. The only way of actually reducing the nitrate level is by water changes.

pH

The action of a biological filter produces acid which always tends to lower the pH level. The decline in pH is due mostly to this factor, so if persistently low pH is a problem then the cause is likely to be the same as those mentioned in *nitrate*. The higher the loading on the filter, the more rapid the drop in pH.

pH has been discussed in previous chapters and details of suitable chemicals to stabilize pH are mentioned.

An interesting fact to bear in mind is that denitrification cancels out, to a large extent, the adverse effects that nitrification has on pH. A system that incorporates a denitrifying or nitrate-inhibiting filter system will not normally suffer from a drop in pH.

Temperature

Temperature should be stable and within the accepted range of 24-30°C (75-86°F). A heater should be set at the maximum temperature which the room is likely to reach. A common mistake is to set the temperature of the aquarium too low. This way the room temperature will keep the tank warm during the day but at night the water temperature will drop to whatever the aquarium thermostat is set at. Although the temperature will not fall too much, it will fluctuate and this often gives rise to disease outbreaks.

Specific gravity

This should be between 1.020 and 1.025. It is not critical but should be kept as constant as possible. It is impossible to keep seaweeds and delicate invertebrates in a constantly varying environment.

Most hydrometers are reasonably accurate but care should be taken. With some of the glass floating type, the paper scale inside the hydrometer can slip and cause huge errors. If in doubt, it is a simple matter to check the reading of your hydrometer with that of a friend.

Redox potential

Very few aquarists possess a redox potential meter (Figure 34) because the cost is prohibitive. However, if you are lucky enough to own one, it can be a most useful instrument. Redox is the potential of reduction or oxidation and is usually measured in rH units; in the marine aquarium it is generally the case that the higher the reading the better.

A high redox potential indicates good breakdown of organic waste whilst a low redox value indicates reduction of the waste to hydrogen sulphide and ammonia.

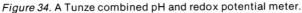

Figure 34. A Tunze combined pH and redox potential meter.

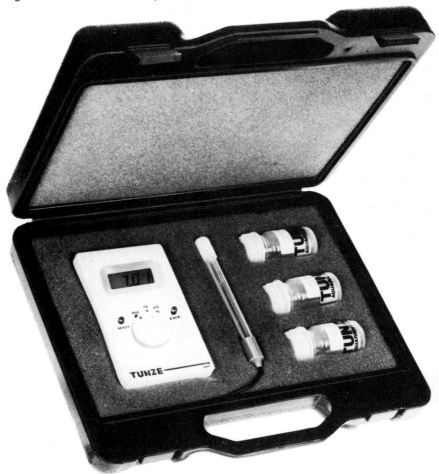

APPENDIX: EQUIPMENT CHART

Photocopy this list and use it to compare the prices of various systems:

tank
hood
stand
base unit/cabinet
heater
thermostat
heater thermostat
mercury vapour lighting
fluorescent tubes
ballast units
under-gravel filters
coral sand
coral gravel
dolomite
crushed shell
other
separating mesh
air pumps
water pumps (power uplifts)
air line etc

power filter
box filter
filter medium
system filter
protein skimmer
osmolator
u/v sterilizer
ozonizer
salt
thermometer
hydrometer
ammonia test kit
nitrite test kit
nitrate test kit
pH test kit
copper test kit
oxygen test kit
redox meter
rocks
coral

USEFUL ADDRESSES

United Kingdom

Aqua Magic Ltd, Marine House, Market Street, Watford, Hertfordshire WD1 7AN (Sole UK distributors of Tunze equipment)

The Aquatic Centre, Golden Vale, Shurdington Road, Brockworth, Gloucester (Retailers of all kinds of fish and associated equipment)

British Marine Aquarists Association, c/o Steve Preston, 16 Fountain Drive, Robbertown, Liversedge, West Yorkshire WF15 7PX

Practical Fishkeeping Magazine, Bretton Court, Bretton, Peterborough (Magazine distributors)

United States of America

International Marine Aquarium Society, c/o James DeBernado, 91 Tulip Avenue, Fc 2, Floral Park, New York 1101

REFERENCES

BOOKS

Spotte, S. (1979) *Seawater Aquariums: the captive environment* Wiley Interscience

Spotte, S. (1979) *Fish and Invertebrate Culture* Wiley Interscience

PERIODICALS

United Kingdom

Aquarium Digest International (Occasional. Tetra Information Centre, 15 Newlay Lane Place, Leeds LS13 2BB)

Practical Fishkeeping (Monthly. EMAP Publications, Bretton Court, Bretton, Peterborough)

The Aquarist and Pondkeeper (Monthly. The Buckley Press, The Butts, Hall Acre, Brentford, Middlesex)

United States of America

Aquarium Digest International (Occasional. Tetra Sales USA, 201 Tabor Road, Morris Plains, New Jersey 07753)

Freshwater and Marine Aquaria (Monthly. 120 West Sierra Madre Boulevard, Sierra Madre, California 91024)

Tropical Fish Hobbyist Magazine (Monthly. TFH Publications Inc., 211 W. Sylvania Avenue, Neptune City, New Jersey 07753)

INDEX

Numbers in *italics* refer to illustrations.